A VICTORIAN BOYHOOD

CRANMER HALL, NORFOLK

After a painting by Felix Kelly

A VICTORIAN BOYHOOD

BY

L. E. JONES

LONDON
MACMILLAN & CO LTD
NEW YORK · ST MARTIN'S PRESS
1955

MACMILLAN AND COMPANY LIMITED
London Bombay Calcutta Madras Melbourne

THE MACMILLAN COMPANY OF CANADA LIMITED
Toronto

ST MARTIN'S PRESS INC
New York

PRINTED IN GREAT BRITAIN

CONTENTS

FRONTISPIECE

CRANMER HALL, NORFOLK
After a painting by Felix Kelly

CHAPTER I

CHILDHOOD

As a child I had no reason to be ashamed of my grandfather; shame crept in only when I was old enough to have opinions of my own about architecture and theology. It is true that his portrait (he had died before I was born) was that of a man who had been unable, or disinclined, to maintain the lustre of his own father and uncles. For they had been painted in military uniforms, with red ribbons and stars and medals; one, indeed, at full length, with the castle of Scylla in the background; another (Napier's 'intrepid Jones') holding a French sword surrendered to him after the fall of San Sebastián where, at the age of sixteen, he had led the forlorn hope. For many years I believed this to mean a desperate adventure undertaken with all but no hope of success, and it was a blow to learn that it was no more than a prosaic military term, borrowed from the Dutch, for a 'detached party'.

But my grandfather had been painted in a black coat and waistcoat, and, worse still, he had, above a short square beard, a shaven upper lip, like Mr. Basham. Mr. Basham was always kind to us children, but we could not like the smell of his fustian clothes, and when he weeded, which was his life, he stuck out a behind almost as big and rounded as those of Boxer and Smart, the cart-horses at the Home Farm. We played round this smooth immensity, a rallying-point on the warm gravel paths, happily enough; but when Mr. Basham stood upright to go to his dinner, and to sleep on a shelf in the potting-shed with his head on a bag of plaited straw, the likeness between his shaven upper lip and that of my grandfather in the portrait gave me a vague uneasiness. When I looked at one, I thought of the other, and I should have liked my grandfather's mouth to have been all his own, not shared, so disquietingly, with Mr. Basham.

I have been told that my grandfather, as a young man, was always laughing, and was known to his friends as 'the Boy', until he met with a disappointment in love, and laughed no more. To cheer him up, perhaps, they told him that his first cousin, Emily, was pining away for love of him, and, unlaughing, he married her. Had Dame Edith Sitwell known my grandmother, she could never have coined the epithet 'Emily-coloured', because my grandmother was colourless. She was pious, depressed, and, to judge from old photographs, looked like a widow from the day of her marriage. Whether it was her piety which prompted her now grave young husband to write a book about the Inerrancy of Scripture, I do not know; but write it he did, and lived to be ashamed of it long before I became ashamed of him. It was in the days when Darwin and Huxley were spreading dangerous thoughts; and from many of the yellowing reviews preserved in an old scrap-book, a reader might think that this youthful and obscure Norfolk squire had preserved, single-handed, the ancient creeds of Christendom. But a baronet was still a baronet in the sixties, with a whiff of wickedness about him, and the Church newspapers were clearly delighted to find a lay champion in so unlikely a quarter. Besides, the book contained one invaluable illustration: a diagram explaining the mystery of the Trinity. My grandfather had been a Wrangler at Cambridge, and had no difficulty in drawing an equilateral triangle, for that, and just that, was the diagram, in the middle of an otherwise blank page. Along one side was written 'The Father'; along another 'The Son'; along the third, 'The Holy Ghost'. There you had it; the Trinity explained. Could anything be more comprehensible, for all the Athanasian Creed?

My grandfather had come by the baronetcy, which got him so favourably reviewed, at the hands of a Turkish bandit, who shot an elder brother dead from behind a rock near Macri 'at a distance of about three yards'. The handsome young Sir Lawrence was travelling in Turkey with a companion named Twopeny, Captain Richard Twopeny (formerly of the 52nd Regiment). An Imaüm (priest), from Xanthus, rode in front, armed with a musket and a girdle of cartridges; then Sir L. Jones, a brace of pistols in holsters; last, Twopeny, unarmed. The Imaüm and his servant had seen some Xebecs skulking about and endeavouring to hide among the bushes ahead. Twopeny said, not thinking much of it at the moment, 'Prepare for a general action'. Jones went to the end of a little valley, full of high bushes, the Imaüm at the 'ready'. No Xebecs. Here the road began to ascend a ravine. 'We momentarily expected an attack,' Twopeny wrote to his brother, Edward Twopeny Esqr. of Woodstock in Kent. 'In a quarter of an hour we came to a fountain surrounded by oak-trees. Said Jones, "We may as well stop to lunch here. If these fellows mean to attack us

we can't escape them; and it is better to fight on a full
stomach than an empty one." "Perhaps," said I, "our
numbers look formidable, and they hardly know how
slightly armed we are." "I can hardly think so little of
Turkish courage," he replied. We were about twenty
minutes at luncheon, discussing the merits of the things
put before us just as usual.' Ten minutes after starting
again, Jones and the servant were shot dead, the Imaüm
from Xanthus disarmed, and Captain Twopeny
wounded by a ball in the left breast and a volley of
slugs, six in the head and seven in the body. But the
Xebecs, having rifled the baggage, marched off 'in
military style', and the Imaüm got Twopeny across a
horse and back to Macri, where Mr. Biliotti, the Tuscan
Consul, received him 'with all the affectionate warmth
of a near relation. Nothing could exceed his kindness,
and the sight and the story made him quite ill.' This
was in November, 1845. By January Captain Twopeny was safely in Rome. 'A little more or less lead in
one's head makes no difference. Two of the slugs buried
themselves in the lower jaw just within the whisker.
These I have; they were extracted with some little pain.'

'Good was derived from the evil of this tragical
adventure.' For Sir Stratford Canning made such a
fuss at Constantinople that the Turkish Government
'for the first time exerted itself' to capture the bandits,
and even, at Sir Stratford's insistence, altered the law
'as to not receiving the evidence of Christians', and
established 'a Court, in which in future the evidence
of Christians would be received'. Captain Twopeny
could have added that in due course the evidence of
Jones' younger brother in favour of Christianity would
also be not unfavourably received.

My grandfather's portrait hung in the Inner Hall, a room lighted, like a ship's saloon, by a sky-light. It had six doors, and a harmonium, and there family prayers were held. It was the thing to look as grave as possible during prayers, and my grandfather looked very grave indeed, book in hand. Because of this gravity, and the upper lip, I never remember wishing him back, or that I had known him. All the same I should have liked, when I was a little older, to have heard from his own lips the story of the permanent prisoner in Norwich Castle. Years ago, a man had been committed to prison for contempt of court by the Assize Judge. A few days later the Judge died suddenly. It seems that nobody but the committing Judge had power to release a prisoner committed for contempt, so nothing could be done, the Judge being dead, but to keep the man in gaol. The man himself, not unnaturally, went mad; but still they kept him there. When it was my grandfather's turn to be High Sheriff, he heard about the case, and to the horror of the officials, did what he had no power to do: he took the man away in a cab and put him into a mental home. Nothing happened to my grandfather; the thing could have been done years before. But it had not been done.

The gardeners, of whom Mr. Basham was third, brought in to family prayers a faint, and the stable-men a stronger, whiff of manure, and sat on slender benches behind the maids. A marble angel, restraining a child from treading upon a serpent, presided, very white, over the shadowy space where the household sat. Our own little wicker chairs, that creaked if we fidgeted, faced the servants; and at the words 'Let us pray' we all rose, turned round, and aimed our rumps at one

another, family against domestics, like the children de-
fying the wolves in *Peter Pan*. This manœuvre seemed
to us to be entirely proper, natural, and religious. I do
not think it could have occurred to any of the Christians kneeling in that Inner Hall that it would be possible
to pray to God standing up, as the Presbyterians do.
Made in His Image, as we were (except Mrs. Pleasance,
the laundrywoman, who was made in the image of a
cottage-loaf), we did not, it must be admitted, make
the best of our divine shapes when praying. It was the
fault, no doubt, of the benches, and of our small chairs,
for being so low; but to One looking down from
Above through the sky-light, the spectacle must have
been, even if endearingly, ridiculous.

Family prayers consisted, naturally, of 'repetitions';
whether they were vain repetitions cannot certainly be
known. It demands an unusual gift of concentration to
throw heart and mind, dynamically, behind an over-
familiar form of words, spoken by a third person; we
children did not attempt it but caught each other's eyes
when a word like 'study' occurred in a collect, to
remind us of our father's study. I cannot answer for
the cook and the maids, or even for Dockerell, the
butler (our warm friend 'Docker', who wore black
side-whiskers); but it seems not unlikely that, at that
early hour of the day, with so much to be done, there
were scattered thoughts beneath the trim lace caps, and
that much, if not all, of those incomparable cadences
carried no further than the range of my father's carrying voice. Indeed, there came a day when the out-door
men begged off; so much cleaning up, they said, spoilt
the morning, and my father readily agreed that, if praying spoilt the morning, the morning must come first.

Nor can we be certain as to Whom those prayers, if any did indeed proceed from a heart, were addressed. The concept of God, as it took shape in the mind of an East Anglian under-housemaid in the year 1890 or thereabouts, may well have differed from all other attempts, at whatever times and places, to realise Deity. We may profess to believe theoretically in Monotheism, but we are, taken in the mass, polytheists, and inevitably so, since we each have, and must have, our private vision of the Unknowable.

We children could be reverent and subdued; we were sensitive to the suggestions of posture, of clasped hands and shut eyes ; but although we ended our evening prayer with

> Keep me, oh keep me, King of Kings,
> Beneath Thine own almighty wings,

I do not remember having any comfort from those wings when frightened in the night. A call to Nanny was more effective, and she alone could dispel the horror of a recurring nightmare of enormous red-faced fishmongers, in blue striped aprons, thronging and hanging over my bed. Our belief in God was implicit, but He bored us rather than interested us, and although we elder ones were genuinely shocked when a younger brother, invited to come and hear some 'Sunday reading', said 'If it's anything about Jethuth, I'd rather not come', we were shocked by his temerity in saying it, not by his point of view, which was secretly our own. We were taken to Church at an early age, but sat with our mother in the galilee, so as to avoid disturbing the congregation when we clattered out before the sermon. Even so, the schoolchildren looked round at us, and, had we been consulted, we should have rather borne with the sermon than with this publicity. But our attendance must have been irregular, because one Rector preached 'at' my mother, taking as his text the story of the Infant Samuel. 'Did Samuel's mother stay at home, and read to him from a Child's Bible? No, *she* took him *with* her to the Temple.'

Some of this Rector's Christian names were Arundel Glastonbury St. John, from which you may envisage him as pale, and High Church, and inclined to saintliness. In truth he was rosy and horsey and neglected the parish. On more than one occasion he forgot it was Sunday; a churchwarden went through the white rectory gate, while the congregation waited, to find the Rector in riding-breeches reading *The Times* and believing the day to be Saturday. Clergymen have to believe things even less likely than that; but this sort of incident made talk, and even we children were aware that the Rector was not taken seriously as a spiritual pastor. We knew, too, that he had bitterly reproached my father for disclosing the faults of a horse to an intending purchaser, thereby getting less money than he had paid for it. But we liked his groom, Mr. Gibbon, and his parlour maid, whose name I have forgotten, and the Rector himself was kindly enough towards us except when we galloped our ponies on the gravelled church-path across the park. We knew that, for the sake of the ponies' legs, it was our business to keep to the grass; but the ponies did not know it, and loved the gravel, and having strong wills and hard mouths, they had their way. The Rector could tell by the spacing of the hoof-marks that there had been galloping, and since bad horsemastership was as sinful in his eyes as telling the truth about a horse for sale, we were scolded as severely as our father had been admonished. All the more, then, were we taken by surprise, and hurt, on an occasion when the Rector betrayed an unsuspected depth of spiritual and religious feeling. There had been infectious illness in the house, and my elder brother and I were sent to sleep for a few nights at the Rectory. The Rector came to our gloomy bedroom to bid us goodnight, and saw on the dressing-table a handful of oats, from one of our pockets, heaped upon a Bible. There was a fearful explosion; his eyes flashed with indignation at such 'irreverence', and all of a sudden he was very much the man of God. We were made to feel very worthless indeed; and I can still remember the sense of injury, for we had intended no insult to our Creator, mingled with a kind of awe at discovering so much hidden holiness in this horsey little man. Clearly we had badly misjudged a Christian priest. His predecessor at the Rectory, Mr. Upcher, whom our father so surprisingly called 'Hay', was a very different type. He had a splendid hooked nose and a black beard, and made us laugh till we ached. But we knew enough to be sure that he would not make jokes in church, and when, at a children's service, he told us that the Church was built of Christian people, and slid his hand up a great stone pier, touching one stone after another, 'here a man, there a woman, here a child', I was amazed. The stones did not seem big enough to contain human bodies, but Mr. Upcher was obviously in earnest, and I could only wonder, and leave it at that, as children do. That a man could be encased in stone after death, we knew, because my great-grandfather, Sir John, had been 'stoned', as we called it, and set up in St. Paul's Cathedral, and an engraving of him in his stone casing hung at the foot of the staircase. But this 'stoning' must have been done with a very thin veneer, or crust, of stone, since every feature showed through, including the curls on his head. Only the eyes were quite smooth and blank and blind. Besides, this treatment of the dead was only used in the case of Generals; other people were buried in the churchyard. Mr. Upcher, to everybody's dismay, suddenly received a long-distance call to be a missionary in Mashonaland; and a marquee was set up on the lawn, with another tent for the tea, and Bishop Knight-Bruce came and addressed the people. And we all had money-boxes with Mr. Upcher's photograph gummed on to them; and a magazine used to arrive with pictures of our dear Mr. Upcher standing among his black catechumens. And young Washington Hammond, the son of one of my father's tenants, was moved to write to Archdeacon Upcher, as he soon became in that sparse mission-field, to ask if he might join him there and preach the gospel to the heathen. But the Archdeacon wrote back that he might come and welcome, but it would be to black the Archdeacon's boots. So young Washy Hammond stayed at home. And when the Archdeacon himself returned, grizzled and twinkling, to revisit his old parish, there were some shakings of the head. 'They du say he smokes *and* drinks' — he, once the leader and inspirer of the local Band of Hope. It was only too true; the good Christian man smoked a pipe, and took a little whisky for his stomach's sake. This was not the first blow dealt to the Band of Hope. My elder brother, in fair white flannels with a broad blue sash across his chest, and myself walking at his pony's shoulder, had ridden through the streets of Fakenham at the head of a procession of teetotal children. It was an afternoon, for me, of almost unbearable shame and shyness, but undeniably, for both of us, a public commitment. And yet my father so far forgot himself as to give us both our first taste of port-wine, under the very eyes of Dockerell, within a few weeks of our formal dedication to life-long abstention. Dockerell was a blue-riband man, and I can still see his pale shocked face. He told us, later, in the pantry, that we had as good as taken the pledge by heading that procession, and what would people think? It was a new idea to us that teetotalism could have anything to do with drinking claret or port. We had understood it to mean not getting drunk on beer in public-houses. And so it was our turn to be shocked by Dockerell for being shocked at anything my father chose to do. For there were still some years to go before I was to be ashamed of my father.

My thoughts have wandered far from family prayers, but the mention of my father reminds me again of the remarkably wide angle through which he could sway, when standing up to read the gospel, without losing his balance. We stood close to his knickerbockers and long thin legs, which oscillated, forwards and back again, to the rhythm of the lovely sentences. Short as we were, when we tried to emulate this fascinating performance we had to shuffle a small foot, to recover balance, long before we had managed a fraction of that masterly sway. It came to have, for us, an almost liturgical significance; it was, literally, a religious exercise. But we never could manage it.

Another thing I never could have managed, or so I then thought, had I been my father, was to read without faltering the verse in the Litany which begins:

B

'That it may please thee to bless and keep the Magistrates'. 'Magistrate' was a word used in a nursery game called 'Greeks and Romans', and after our nurses had explained that a magistrate was something our father was, I could have died with shame, in his shoes, before praying for myself out loud before all the servants. Even as a diminutive child of a magistrate, I felt involved in the embarrassment; and dreaded, while the illumination of the Bishops, Priests and Deacons, and the endowment of the Nobility, were being besought for, the inevitable moment when we Magistrates were to be brought, so clearly and loudly, to the notice of God and the maids.

Family prayers yielded one rather singular benefit to our primitive consciousness. We found there a kind of weather-forecast for the day, or at any rate for the morning hours. The sign was in the frock worn by my mother, as she sat at the harmonium. It was our first sight of her; and if she wore a plaid skirt, the morning would be dull but fair. Was she in a certain brown dress, we must expect tears before luncheon; but if she appeared in muslin, or anything frilly or flowery, all would be fun and gaiety for the rest of the day. Did her clothes really affect my mother's moods, as we firmly believed? Or was it that her mood, on rising, determined her choice of frocks? Whatever the explanation our meteorological office seemed to us, upon the whole, wonderfully dependable.

The significance of this mother-weather lay in the fact that our mother was also our governess. This was partly for economy, but more because my parents had theories about education. It is true that a German nursery-governess had once been engaged, but she pro-

nounced 'wir wollen'as 'wire woolen', and turned out
to be only an Australian and so left us again after a few
days, much to our disgust. For she had once been given
a towel to bite, and while biting the towel had had both
eyes taken out, scraped, and put back again. Her eyes
were very blue, as a result, no doubt, of the scraping,
and her hair bright yellow, and she wore a check blouse
with a large cameo brooch. She had seen cockatoos
flying from tree to tree, not to speak of kangaroos, and
it seemed to us a shame that so exciting a newcomer
should be asked to pack her bags so soon. It was a
notable instance of the mysteriously mistaken values of
grown-ups.

Lessons were delightful when my mother wore a
summer frock, and we used to clap our hands and jump
when Poitiers was won so soon after Crécy. And we
were thrilled, knowing that all would come right again,
to learn that never had the fortunes of England sunk to
a lower ebb than at the moment when Queen Elizabeth
mounted the throne. My mother read aloud beauti-
fully, and was not afraid of using books rather above
our heads; new words were looked out in Skeat's
Etymological Dictionary and their derivations discussed,
and we were set to frame sentences of our own in which
the difficult word ('abrupt' comes back to my mind)
was to be given its proper place and meaning.

But if the brown frock, or some other dress giving
warning of a depression over Iceland, was being worn,
there would be, more likely than not, tears over the
participe passé. An unfortunate younger brother, indeed,
never could form the most shadowy conception of what
the *participe passé* was, and eventually had to go into the
Navy. As for music-lessons, tears were the rule; for

my mother suffered excruciatingly from wrong notes, and our small hands were knocked off the keyboard by that instrument of torture — a grown-up hand wearing rings. Music-teachers should either be tone-deaf, or patient, or take off their rings before the lesson begins.

On the whole, I am convinced that mothers should not be governesses, any more than the American Constitution should have combined the offices of President and Prime Minister in one person. There should be room for an appeal from governess to parent; and when the gong goes for luncheon — possibly the most delectable sound in the world — it should be a signal of absolute release, not of an immediate re-encounter between the school room combatants. At the moment of reproof, or correction, children 'hate' the reprover, and haters and hated ought not to lunch together. But we children lunched downstairs from a very early age, and had not always had time, while washing our hands and faces, to re-orientate our feelings towards the impatient autocrat of the schoolroom.

My father came into the schoolroom, at a later stage, to teach us Latin. He had a double share of my mother's natural impatience, and none of her undoubted gift for teaching, and for arousing our interest in the matter in hand. Latin lessons were apt to break up suddenly, with the book thrown down and my father washing his hands of us as unteachable. We were, doubtless, irritating. In the first stages of learning Latin there is a constant preoccupation with two Roman ladies, Julia and Cornelia, who take it in turns to adorn the table with roses. Julia gave no trouble; but, with our atavistic English dislike of prolonged or unnecessary articulation, we insisted on referring to her colleague as C'nelia. 'CORNelia!',

my father would roar; but we could not frame our
tongues to it. It seemed to be against nature to give so
much importance to the first syllable of a four-syllabled
word, and we would not, or rather could not, docile as
we were, accomplish the thing twice running. This
exasperated him, while for our part we thought he made
a great fuss about nothing; time was wasted, and authority weakened. It never seems to have occurred to him
to let Julia do all the table-decorations off her own bat.
As for algebra, we defeated him entirely. He chalked
$A \times B$, $A + B$, and $A - B$ on the blackboard, and explained that we were now to learn the art of multiply-
ing, not number by number, but letter by letter, and of
adding and subtracting letters to and from each other.
We pointed out that this was impossible. 'A times B'
meant nothing at all. When he went on to explain that
A stood for a number, but that it was an unknown
quantity, we replied that, if it was unknown, nothing
could be done about it. My father had the sense to see
that we were so profoundly convinced of our rightness
that further argument would be useless, and algebra
was, literally, laughed out of court. For we were
genuinely amused at this preposterous branch of learning, and my father, always open to new ideas, from
whatever source, joined in the laughter.

But Green's *Short History of the English People* and
the *Latin Primer*, and even the great Skeat himself, could
not in themselves have laid the foundations of an
aesthetic sense, and a delight in Georgian architecture,
so keen as to cause their possessor to be profoundly
ashamed of the grandfather who played the devil with
Cranmer Hall. Poetry must come into the story, and
letters; and, above all, since nobody can look at a

Georgian building and love it without a sense of right and wrong, morals.

There was also, in my own case, the negative necessity of being first cured of military ambition. Soldiers are fine fellows, but personal loyalty — 'my grandfather right or wrong' — is an essential part of their make-up; their squadron, their regiment, is always the best in the British Army, and long may this be so, since the stresses of battle call for irrational faith as well as for clearness of sight. (It is true that the Duke of Wellington, in taking my great-grandfather over the field of Waterloo, said: 'In fact, there was so much misbehaviour, that it was only through God's mercy that we won the battle', but then the Duke of Wellington was many things besides a soldier.) In my childhood I was as much in love with military glory as any Churchill. We children had lived double lives from as far back in time as I can remember; the full, vivid lives, taking up most of our play-time, of Prince Willy and Prince Miller. I was Prince Miller until a day when Miller suddenly took on a bourgeois, unprincely sound, and we decided, well knowing that we were humbugging ourselves, that it had all along been short for Émile. But these young princes were not soldiers; they walked in green with silver swans embroidered on their chests, and their sport was hunting, or shooting with bows and arrows. Their most onerous undertaking was the journey from the Winter to the Summer Palace in May, and from the Summer back to the Winter Palace in October. The route of this royal progress was the complete circuit of the Home Farm, through a belt of Scotch firs; there was good enough stag-hunting to be had on the way, but it was a mile and a half long, at the least;

and during the last, aching, dragging half-mile home to tea in the Winter (or Summer) Palace, the deer, and even the occasional wild-boar, were not much molested.

But the *Lances of Lynwood* made an end of all that childishness. Bertrand du Guesclin, the ugliest and bravest knight of them all, could not co-exist with the 'hindward feather and the forward toe' of Prince Miller. If he had lived a double life before the coming of the Lances, it was all but a single life now. Crécy and Poitiers during lessons; Michael Drayton's 'Battle of Agincourt' chanted or shouted behind the yew hedges; in or out of the schoolroom the excitement was continuous. Wooden swords were dipped into a pot of red paint that was kept in the seed-room ; a younger brother died many times over, not always painlessly, as the Borne Basque. Our secular foes were, of course, the French.

> Exeter had the rear,
> A braver man not there ;
> O Lord, how hot they were
> On the false Frenchmen!

And when a false Frenchman appeared in person to teach us French, while himself learning English, he needed more good-nature and tolerance than most of us possess to face up to our Francophobia. But dear Monsieur Georges Deloche de Noyelle never winced; at the most he asked us to give Agincourt the French pronunciation, as we did to Crécy and Poitiers. He had his revenge, all the same; for he dug out from a high shelf in the library a splendid volume bound in red and gold, called *Jeanne d'Arc*, illustrated with countless battle-pieces in which the English were always, shamefully and unaccountably, but undeniably, running away.

Fortunately I so fell in love with a coloured picture of
Jeanne herself, with the face of an angel and wavy
golden hair, clad in shining armour and white surcoat,
mounted on a prancing white horse and holding up the
most gloriously-named banner in history, the Ori-
flamme, — I fell so deeply in love with this adorable
person that I forgot my shame. Who would not surrender to, rather than fight with, such loveliness?

And in the end Georges, with his 'grands yeux bis',
as I called them (to his puzzlement, till I argued that
since 'pain bis' meant brown bread, 'bis' must be the
French for 'brown') added fuel to the flames of my
soldierly ambitions. For with the curiosity of a stranger,
he poked about in the library, and interested us, for the
first time, in the careers of Sir John and Sir Harry and
Captain George, R.N., whose portraits glowed from
the walls of the Entrance Hall. He did not take them
for granted, as we had taken them; and he knew
enough about dates to point out that for Sir Harry to
have distinguished himself in both the Peninsular and
Crimean wars was quite a thing. And he discovered
why the stone coat-of-arms on the pediment of the
blind façade of our home (blinded with plate-glass by
my grandfather, alas) had the word 'Netherlands'
upon it, and why the lion had a medal round his neck
inscribed 'Badajos', although he failed to explain why
the lion's tail was curled inside his hind leg as he
crouched. Living as we did in the age of chivalry, we
had cared nothing for these memorials of modern war-
fare. But there was a lock of Napoleon's hair, cut off
after death, in the glass-topped treasure table in the
drawing-room, and there were letters from the Duke
of Wellington to Sir John. And Monsieur Georges,

gallantly (for it added Salamanca and Toulouse and Waterloo to the list of French defeats which we loved to recite at the breakfast-table), showed us these things, and lifted us clean out of the fourteenth century to set us down in the early part of the nineteenth, wearing red coats and epaulettes, and avid for command. Command: that was the function for which I already felt myself to be secretly ready; and I still see the exact spot, among the periwinkles behind the Summer-house, where I practised those attitudes which, in a commander, must become second nature. With one foot raised and planted upon an out-cropping root of the lime-tree, right hand on hip, chin up, I stood, rigid with authority, and whistled. I have never seen a general whistle on parade, but in those days I had not seen soldiers at all in the flesh; and there is no doubt that whistling does give to the whistler a scornful, superior look of unconcern, which could well — who knows? — impress the troops.

It must also have been about this time that I had a recurring dream, repeating itself in each sharp detail, in which I died, shot through the chest, on the field of battle, in the moment of victory. I subsided into the arms of an officer; the anxious staff, red-coated and gold-braided, hung over me; I knew that the battle was won and that the credit of it was mine; and then I woke up. Dreams, as well as day-dreams, pointed to a splendid, possibly a heroic, career.

That I should some day be shot through the chest turned out to be true enough, but there were then no aides-de-camp's arms to break my fall, the British Army was in full retreat, and I was not in command of it. But I was not to know that; and being sensible enough to realise that even those of us born to command must begin at the bottom, I decided to consult Mr. Walker upon the first steps to be taken.

Mr. Walker was an under-gardener, but had served his time as a soldier, a 'private' soldier, which sounded to me rather select and exclusive. His Christian name was Elijah, which we felt to be faintly irreverent, but he justified this presumption by occasionally preaching in the tiny chapel in which, our mother told us, people could be, rather surprisingly, as good Christians as in church. Mr. Walker had a red beard, and was busy trenching celery in the dull stretch of kitchen-garden by the potting-shed on the fateful day when he destroyed, at a blow and for ever, my splendid aspirations.

The conversation began well enough, with the choice of a regiment. Mr. Walker had served in the Norfolks, but had the detachment not to insist that his own was the only regiment worthy of my consideration. In fact, he did not hesitate. The Lancers, he said, were the thing for me (we did not go into the niceties of weighing the 5th against the 9th or the 12th, the 16th or 17th against the 21st). Planting his spade firmly into the wormy soil, so as to leave both hands free, he described in the air an isosceles triangle, with its apex turned down. I have forgotten with what red or yellow, or blue or gold, this triangle was so resplendent; but it represented that part of a lancer's uniform which would cover my chest, and he easily persuaded me that there was no more beautiful chest-covering in the whole British Army. The lance, too, was a dashing weapon, and a familiar one; for I had handled it skilfully in my Lynwood days, wearing the pennon of a Knight-banneret (which, as everybody knows, gave me pre-

cedence over all Knights-bachelor). A day did come,
indeed, when Mr. Walker's choice for me was fulfilled;
there were crossed lances on my Yeomanry buttons
even when my weapon was a Vickers machine-gun;
but Mr. Walker, happily for himself, did not live to
know that in my regiment's armoury there were but
half a dozen lances, used for tent-pegging.

The regiment decided upon, I came to my main
point, the question of promotion. To my surprise,
Mr. Walker saw no advantages in the privacy of a
'private' soldier. I was to start as an officer. I became
a Captain in no time, and a Major in Mr. Walker's next
breath, and almost immediately afterwards as fine a
gentleman (we both hoped) as Mr. Walker's own
Colonel had been. My spell as a brigadier-general took
longer, since the meaning of a brigade had to be explained, but, that grasped, I rose rapidly to Major-
General and commanded, hand on hip, a division. In
my ignorance I was not in a position to pose Mr.
Walker with the problem, which so puzzled me in the
First World War, as to how brigadiers who, in that
war at least, had thick red necks, were able to achieve,
on promotion, the thin pale necks, with a slight vertical
depression running down them, which were the dis-
tinctive physical signs of a divisional commander. But
I feel sure he could not have given me an answer which
only generals can know, and have never told. What
he could answer, readily enough, when we came to the
next upward step, was my question why, since a major
is much grander than a lieutenant, a major-general is
less grand than a lieutenant-general. It did not seem to
me to make sense, besides demanding mental effort, if
one was to keep a firm hold of the rungs on the ladder

to command. But Mr. Walker explained that the reason for the apparent anomaly was that a lieut.-General is of higher rank than a major-general. And with that I had to be content, with the same faint inner disquietude with which, in earlier years, I had accepted an aunt's statement that she had been to Palestine. Palestine, as the scene of our Lord's life, was at that time confused in my mind with Paradise; and I could neither disbelieve a grown-up aunt, nor quite believe that she had been there. Mr. Walker, as a soldier, must know ; but his reasoning bothered me.

Promoted full General, I believed myself to be within one step of my destiny and was taken aback to learn, for the first time, of the existence of Field-Marshals. Mr. Walker lingered lovingly over these, and told me that Lord Wolseley was the greatest soldier of them all. Then was he the Commander-in-Chief? I asked.

Then and there the blow fell. 'Nobody,' said Mr. Walker, 'can be Commander-in-Chief except His Royal Highness himself.' All was over; a military career, so ardently looked forward to, was not for me. There was no future in it. Yet Mr. Walker, hitherto so sympathetic, having destroyed a noble ambition in a couple of seconds, took up his spade and calmly went on trenching celery. That stretch of kitchen-garden beyond the potting-shed looked not merely dull, it looked dreary.

There is nothing surprising in the fact that, in the early nineties, Mr. Walker should have regarded H.R.H. the Duke of Cambridge [1] as immortal, or at any rate

[1] Better known to the present generation, thanks to Mr. Laurence Housman, as the Duke of Flamborough. Perfection is a strong word and a rare thing, but in the Duke of Flamborough's farewell speech to the army it is, I think, to be found.

believed that royal birth was a necessary qualification for the post of Commander-in-Chief. What is surprising is that I should have accepted the extinction of all my hopes from an under-gardener, without asking for corroboration from any other grown-up person. But such thoughts as mine were not to be confided to anybody. Self-aggrandizement in any form was as repellent to our common social sense as it was obsessive in my private soul. I should have hooted at my elder brother, the companion of my days and nights, had he pretended to the mildest hopes of ultimate success in life, and he would have hooted at me. We were inseparable; we were necessary to one another; we compared notes on everything external; but our hearts' secrets were locked.

As to my parents, I knew that they did not take my military ambitions seriously. If there was to be a soldier in my generation, it would naturally be my elder brother. A phrenologist in a side-show at the Royal Aquarium, to whom my father, who possessed the most uncritical and receptive of minds, had taken us when very small boys indeed, had pronounced my brother to have a strong bump of 'combativeness', and recommended the army as a career. When my turn came, and my bumps had been investigated, it was humiliation and disappointment for me. No signs of generalship. 'Literary tendencies.' I hardly understood the word, but my father explained, still jaunty and amused, and I was bitterly hurt. To be only a soldier's brother; to be destined to write, not fight. It was hardly to be borne. Had the phrenologist divined the truth, that my professional career was to be that of an Investment Banker, I think even my father, had he then understood the term, would have been taken aback. As for myself, to this very day I have a secret belief that a very good general indeed has been lost to the world; not a Commander-in-Chief, not a strategist, not a master of logistics, but the very devil of a fellow for appreciating a tactical situation, and for attacking, attacking.

Well, Mr. Walker put an end to all that. And so elastic is youth, so protean the ego of a small boy, that it cannot have been long after the realisation that I was to be for ever stymied by the bulk of His Royal Highness, that my ambition took a surprisingly different turn. It was some visitor, I think, who asked us all at luncheon what we hoped to be. 'A soldier', said my elder brother. 'A sailor,' said a younger one. I said nothing. I was pressed, but refused to answer. 'Had I not made up my mind?' No, my mind was made up, but I couldn't possibly tell it. I grew red in the face. My mother noticed my embarrassment, and changed the subject. After luncheon, my mother captured me; we stood together on the little orange-coloured mat that protected the drawing-room door from draughts, and she besought me to whisper, in her secret ear, my life's objective. I held out stubbornly, feeling acutely the shamefulness of my choice; but she persisted and, trusting in her promise not to betray me, I at length, miserably, let my foolish little cat out of the bag. 'The Poet Laureate.' I cannot say that my mother encouraged me, but she did not laugh at me, and even went so far as to say that it was not an ignoble ambition. Poets were not necessarily unmanly, she said, or soft; look at Lord Tennyson. It was not my choice, but my shame about it, out of which she tried to reason me. It remained a secret between her and me; and to this day I cannot account for my obstinate, if temporary, determination to become an Alfred Austin. We had all got by heart, as a part of our lessons, a good deal of verse, beginning with Mrs. Margaret Woods' *First Poetry Book* and working up to Henley's *Lyra Heroica* and Andrew Lang's *Blue Poetry Book*. We enjoyed spouting 'The Revenge', 'Lars Porsena', and the 'Battle of Lake Regillus'; and my favourite poems for private reading were Poe's 'Annabel Lee', and 'Ulalume', and the fascinating piece by W. M. Praed called 'The Devil's Decoy':

> There was turning of keys and creaking of locks
> As he took forth a bait from his iron box.

But our own compositions were worthless puerilities about robins and Nature. Can the real reason for my vaulting ambition have been that there is only one Poet Laureate? Might not he also, in his solitariness, have stood, chin in air, and whistled?

I think the dubious associations in my mind with the word 'Poet', which made my new-chosen profession so sickeningly difficult to avow, must have been the fault of Wordsworth and Blake. In earlier days we had been taught to recite 'Little lamb, who made thee?', and to recite it with proper feeling. I thought it degradingly babyish; besides, it re-echoed the discomforts of the last part of the Litany and that most embarrassing of symbolic figures, the Lamb of God. Lambing-time on the Home Farm was always an excitement for us; we loved the straw shelters set up to protect my father's — or rather, Mr. Olley, the bailiff's — Southdown ewes and lambs from the devilish Norfolk east winds; and we could be most tender-minded and loving towards the lambs themselves. But we saw them in their extreme

youth, with legs too big for their bodies and the
umbilical cord still raw, and, dear as they were, it was
absurd to conceive of one of these flop-eared, moist
babies as taking away the Sins of the World. If church-
men only knew the minds of children, they would
surely be the first to protect the strength of their imperi-
ous Saviour from this debilitating image! But then,
had they known the minds of children, they could
never have compelled them to sing:

> We are but little children weak,

with a strangled resentment against a religion which,
like Blake's poem, exalted meekness and mildness.
Little children are tough customers and, to themselves,
the future masters of circumstance, and they will never
be attracted to Jesus until He is set before them as He
was, the First of Heroes.

'Nurse's Song' also did Blake no good in my eyes.
Their own voices heard on the green can have no
pathetic or tender overtones for children, and 'the little
ones leapt, and shouted, and laughed' gave me a picture
of absurd, meaningless caperings. It was a distasteful
poem, and I wondered at my mother's affection for such
stuff. Wordsworth's 'We are Seven' and 'The Pet
Lamb' I found equally objectionable, and was only able
to 'take' 'Lucy Gray', as we moderns say, because of
two lines which enchanted me:

> The minster-clock has just struck two,
> And yonder is the moon!

I heard the clock; I saw the moon; I was thrilled at the
conjunction. Our home had a clock-tower (designed
for my grandfather by Philip Webb), and it may have
been the well-known pleasure of subconscious recognition which so endeared those lines to me, as also, in

maturer days, a line of Meredith's in which I found magic:

> The hall-clock holds the valley on the hour.

The children that interest children are not 'the little ones' of loving mothers and nurses, or Wordsworth's anaemic little girls; they are the rowdy boys in Louisa Alcott's *Little Men* or the brave treasure-seekers of E. Nesbit. *Songs of Innocence* are far removed from the spirit of lusty, combative childhood; and it would be doing a service to Blake and Wordsworth to keep them hidden away from infant philistines. Blake, in particular, should be reserved, like savings, for a rainy day; to be suddenly loosed, a shaft of light from a stormy sky, upon the creeping dullness of sophistication.

The Poet Laureate, in whose shoes I so strangely aspired to stand, was Tennyson; and while I could and did relish the splendour of

> The stars are from their hands
> Flung through the woods,

it was 'The Revenge' that made his glory and mine. Little boys like strong meat when they can get it, and battle and murder and sudden death were not so easy to come by in our nonage. My mother was all for sweetness and light; her copy of Matthew Arnold shows favourite passages faintly marked in pencil; and our reading was rigorously overlooked. But Mrs. Mortimer's *Far Off, or Asia described,* in faded orange covers, was a lesson book, and while its companion, *Near Home, or Europe described*, was tantalisingly disfigured with blacked-out passages (relating, I was told in after years, to God's anger with the Roman Catholics for worshipping a woman and a piece of bread), *Far Off* had escaped the censor's ink. 'Horrible as were the

c

massacrees of Lucknow, still more horrible were the massacrees of Cawnpory.' What more promising chapter-
opening could a small boy want? All the same, I cannot have been wholly a savage, or without a sense of
decorum, for I can remember being genuinely shocked
at the words inscribed by Mrs. Pollyhampton (spelt
Polehampton) on the tombstone of her husband and
child. The Reverend Mr. Pollyhampton, together
with his only child, had been murdered by sepoys and
thrown down a well, and his widow had caused the
following inscription to be graved upon their head-
stone:

'IS IT WELL WITH THY HUSBAND?
IS IT WELL WITH THY CHILD?'
AND SHE ANSWERED 'IT IS WELL.'

It never crossed my mind that she had not intended a
pun, and I felt that, in the tragic circumstances, she
ought to have resisted it.

A still more extraordinary case of the censor's blind-
ness was a short tale at the end of a thick, blue *First
Reading Book*, intended for very small children indeed,
where 'the bones and blood' of a child eaten by a wolf
are described with the relish we lately reserved for
the sinking of a German U-boat. I daresay the child
was eaten for an act of disobedience; but the moral is
forgotten while the agreeable shudder abides.

Those were the days when 'improving' books were
still being put into the hands of the little ones, and it is
a tribute to Maria Edgeworth's skill in telling a story
that she was able to hoodwink us into supporting
Rosamund's mother — that monster of judicial aloofness — against Rosamund's simplicity. A word of
warning could have saved Rosamund's pocket-money

and self-respect alike, and modern mothers are alert to give it; but we little ones shared in Rosamund's mother's devilish satisfaction in the cold-blooded snaring of the innocent. That no Purple Jar would ever take us in, we felt certain; it was cunning Miss Edgeworth who did that. As for 'The Party of Pleasure', the very name of the story excited me like a roll of drums. I, too, counted all the heads of the Misses Bliss in the carriage, and none of that day's disasters could ever persuade me that a Party of Pleasure, if ever it came my way, would not be a very heaven upon earth.

Evenings at Home was heavier going. We read and re-read that fat, smug, blue-and-gold book for lack of anything else, but the tea-table conversations between Tut. and Pup. as to the provenance of lump-sugar were dreary enough, and the priggish victory of Eyes over No-Eyes got no cheers from me. Yet, even here, there was gold to be extracted, since 'Presence of Mind' began with a lady being bled into a basin; and included a Bengal Tiger who bounded into a Garden Party, and was only prevented from eating the Sahibs by a present-minded lady who opened her parasol in its face.

But those were early days; and while reading to ourselves was regarded by us all as a normal and necessary department of living, literature swam into our ken through reading aloud. It was our mother's reading of *The Water-Babies* that first brought home to me that the charm of a story can be enhanced by the way it is told. True, the crisp colloquialisms of *Tales from the Norse* had surprised and delighted us, after the more even-paced Grimm and the faintly disconcerting sentimentalities of Hans Andersen. Grimm could at moments rise to the height of 'Away they went over stock and stone till their hair whistled in the wind' which made me wriggle with pleasure, but the briskness of 'Yes, the lad would do that' and such repetitions as 'one to hammer and one to hold' were more pervasive and better sustained in the Norse stories.

If the opening chapters of *The Water-Babies* do not rouse even a child to an awareness of style as well as story, it must be supposed that nothing will. Here is the lilt, the rapidity, that makes the reader, and the listener still more closely, captive. He is led from sentence to sentence; there can be no stopping by the way; the story has it all the time; yet the background images are so precise, so luminous, so full of gusto and observation, that not one but adds to the excitement and versimilitude of the tale itself. We had never seen limestone Fells, or an old cock-grouse, or bull-pups carried in a man's pocket, but when Kingsley wrote 'as smart as a gardener's dog on Sunday, with a polyanthus in his mouth' we knew that we could trust him. For it was the habit of our own head gardener, 'Master', to walk the mile and a half from the village every Sunday afternoon, in order to saunter, in a starched dickey and without a neck-tie, through the walled gardens. And at his heels Judy, a brindled mongrel with hair hanging over her brown eyes, carried, in her moist jaws, the very polyanthus of the story. How did Charles Kingsley know that? We could not tell; but know it he did, and we were astonished at his omniscience.

So when Kingsley told us to get up at three o'clock on Midsummer Morning, we obeyed him; and there is evidence of my tender years, or prolonged innocence, in the fact that the first time we did so I was rewarded, as I more than half expected to be, by seeing a fairy.

She was a wisp of a thing not more than two inches in
height, sliding down the coping of the coal-house in
the stable-yard, and I saw her from my bedroom window as I buckled a leather belt round the blue knee-
length blouse which was our everyday dress. But
although the three o'clock rule was kept for some years,
we never saw a fairy again; and when visiting grown-
ups, to whom we liked to report the affair, exchanged
smiles, we began to lose faith ourselves, and hastened
to change the subject, entertaining our lady visitors
instead with the curious fact that bullocks were the only
examples of the neuter gender in living things, and that
one of the geese laid clear eggs, which could never
be hatched, because the gander refused to walk about
with her. No smiles were exchanged over such dry
scientific talk as this; but there came a day when our
father overheard us instructing an aunt in these country
matters and took us apart. He wisely disdained the
fantasy that bullocks were the calves' uncles, and boldly
explained castration, telling us that it would never do
to have the park full of bulls, tossing people and fighting one another. He added, and we saw his point, that
castration was no longer to be a breakfast-table topic.
But he said nothing about the gander.

If Kingsley gave us our first taste of style, Juliana
Horatia Ewing came hard upon his heels. 'Here, bound
up in a paper cover, and nearly overlooked, we found
the book of the season.' So was a reviewer quoted, in
small print, on the back of that paper cover, and for a
second time, when my mother read *Jackanapes* aloud in
her lively, spirited manner, I felt the spell of literature.
This was not just writing; this was the human voice
speaking through the printed word. A woman's voice,

but cool, clear, and amused; knowing boys and knowing soldiers; never telling you to laugh or to cry, but telling you things just as they happened, and leaving you to laugh or choke, not at things in a book, but at things in themselves. I could not know that this was high artistry, but I did know that here was high enjoyment, even when it meant choking; and I was able to recognise that Juliana's voice, her way of saying things, that light, unconcerned tone of hers, and the sentences that ran to the inevitable stopping-place, had all their part in my pleasure. After *Jackanapes*, *Mary's Meadow*, which sent us back to our own unweeded gardens, and after *Mary's Meadow* the *Story of a Short Life*. In this book, it must be admitted, Mrs. Ewing twists life to extract the sentiment, and at times sacrifices art to edification. But we were accustomed to 'uplift', as I shall tell, and preferred it with sugar, however cloying, to taking it neat. So even the 'Brave poor things' could not destroy our pleasure in this too consciously moving tale; and to a conventionally-minded small boy, who would have rather died than make himself conspicuous, the episode of the V.C. who sang alone, outside the tin tabernacle, to please a dying cripple, was as fascinating as it was agonising. As the moment approached for the V.C. to leave his seat, I could hardly bear it for him; I lost all my sympathy for Leonard, who had dared to ask for so unheard of a sacrifice; I felt the burning shame of it, but knew it, as well, for the supreme act of courage. Mrs. Ewing had me down, angry, resentful, and admiring; and, by God, she rubbed it in!

It was Juliana's mother, Mrs. Gatty, who had broken us in to 'uplift'. Her *Parables from Nature* counted as

'Sunday reading'; they were the pudding that followed upon the meat of *The Child's Bible* or *Jesus the Carpenter of Nazareth*. We knew that God and Jesus were tremendous Beings above the sky from whom escape was impossible; there they were, Sunday was Their day, and we must make the best of Them. But to children, as the French editor said when he returned a religious contribution: 'Question de Dieu, cela manque d'actualité'. The towering figure of Jesus, in particular, was so traduced in presentation, diminished to such unheroic proportions, that our imaginations, nourished upon valour and the banners of chivalry, recoiled from Him in boredom. We knew enough to disguise it, but we would rather have listened to any book but *The Carpenter*, with the single exception of Mrs. Barbauld's *Hymns in Prose*. Why this nauseating book was in my mother's Sunday repertory, I cannot tell. I have not seen it since those days, and it cannot have been trash; I only know that the sight of its greeny-brown cover, lying on my mother's lap, made my young heart sink. I have but the vaguest recollection of the hymns themselves; they seemed to me to go with the name Mrs. Barbauld; an outlandish name; a greeny-brown, Sunday kind of name. Name and book, I loathed the pair of them.

Parables from Nature, on the other hand, came to us as a welcome second course. Our favourite story, and my mother's, was called 'Purring when you're pleased'. Englishmen do not often purr when they are pleased, and it is one of the pleasures of travel in the Latin countries to watch men and women doing so. Experience has not altered my opinion that my mother was right to inculcate and to encourage that habit of purring; but she went much further than Mrs. Gatty, for she expected, and even commanded, us to purr when we were not pleased.

That children must be taught a kind of 'white' hypocrisy is certain; society and good manners depend upon it, and it stands high among the virtues which enable our ruthless egos to rub along with one another. It is the virtue lacking in the 'enfant terrible', in the candid friend, in aunts and uncles, and other disrupters of comity. To practise it demands discipline and training, as well as kindly feelings; but if the good feeling is not there, if the impulse to deceive is not spontaneous and charitable, white hypocrisy, that fine blossom of civilisation, turns into odious humbug. A character in *Mary's Meadow*, the big-headed Christopher who drank so much toast-and-water at Lady Catherine's luncheon table, had a saying: 'Doings first, feelings afterwards'. It may be that my mother, too, believed that outward and visible signs would of themselves beget inward and spiritual graces. However that may be, we were made to purr, or to wag our tails, whatever the weather in our small souls. What, for example, can be more dreary for young Princes and Princesses, accustomed to the swiftness of white steeds, than to be driven, in a low, yellowish pony-cart, between the brambly, dusty hedges of a country lane? 'Mite', the Shetland pony, was over thirty years old, and did not care for 'nice drives' any more than we did; yet a 'nice drive' it had to be, when suddenly decreed at the luncheon-table. And if rain threatened, we even had to wear our 'nice'capes, which scratched our chins and necks, and reminded me sickeningly, by their colour, of the pink and white pips in the entrails of a young mouse on whom I had trodden by the haystack. It was not enough to accept the word 'nice' from my mother with cheerful looks; we had formally to withdraw the word 'beastly' as being un-parliamentary, and to aver that 'nice' was the proper and appropriate description of both drive and capes.

Another rule in the discipline of white hypocrisy was that, whatever our ploys or games out of doors, in the garden or on the Home Farm, at the first appear-ance of a Parent we must down tools, or swords, or spears, and run, with love and eagerness in our faces, to greet him or her. Nobody likes to be interrupted; and the chances are that in breaking in upon children you are jolting not merely an occupation but a day-dream. You come upon them, not from the kitchen-garden, but from a prosaic world from which they are temporarily seeking asylum. And the disturbance is aggravated when the tall parental figures appear at the farthest end of the terrace or, worse still, coming across the park from Fox-hill or the Primrose Walk. That meant a long run for short legs; but our dark blue blouses under wide straw hats, or red tam-o'-shanters, were easily spotted from afar, and if they could see us, it would be no good pretending that we had not seen them. So run we must, pumping up eagerness from nowhere as best we could, and enchanting my mother, I have no doubt, by this evidence of our ever-loving hearts.

It was the same thing with Church; it was the same with Sunday reading; it was the same with going in the carriage. Invited to volunteer for these dreary occa-sions, we vied with each other in being the most for-ward; and it is still a puzzle to me how my mother, so reproachful to a hanger-back, could yet be taken in, as she undoubtedly was, by our calculated pretences of enjoyment. I am sorry I did not discuss it with her when, in later years, she became my dearest friend. I must remember to do so in the Elysian fields.

I do not think this system was successful. The great gulf that separates truthfulness from candour is not apparent to young moralists, and, once relieved from the day-to-day pressure of my mother's platinum will-power, I, for my part, relapsed into the unpalatable practices of candour with all the more abandon for having been so long restrained. For Truthfulness itself, in the limited sense of speaking the truth, had never had a place in our moral training; to tell the truth on all occasions was not something you ought to do, or had to do, it was something you did, like eating or breathing. Sins and naughtiness were such things as 'Me first!', greediness, quarrelling, violence, rudeness, unkindness, and so on; and when our youngest brother told the first untruth in the history of the family, we felt as normal men and women sometimes feel towards perversion. My father beat him with a withy in the bathroom, and we went about with hushed voices. In after years it was discovered that Maurice was often genuinely unable to distinguish between fact and day-dream, and he went into the Church.

How a child constitutionally incapable of lying is to be taught the social graces, I do not know. But I feel sure that at any rate his natural affections should never be put under pressure; no welcome demanded, no kiss bespoken as of right. For myself, I disliked physical contacts of all kinds, except kissing a kitten's forehead or rubbing against my cheek the smooth, cool curves of an ivory paper-knife. To be caressed by a grown-up person turned me sour; and I am convinced that serious damage may be done to young affections by lack of respect for bodily aloofness.

My mother dedicated the whole of her great heart and considerable intelligence to the task of making us healthy, happy, and above all things, good. Dignified and abnormally shy and reticent in social relationships, loved and feared by faithful Norfolk retainers, she set about moulding us to her will with single-minded vigour, uninterrupted by worldly concerns. She could be gay and amused; she loved to make us laugh; and she encouraged us to be physically adventurous and hardy. Having no governess but herself, we were masters of our play-times, and our freedom to roam was absolute. But her watchfulness for faults of character, of behaviour, of manners, of deportment, was close and unremitting. No lapse ever went undetected or unreproved; we were asked, after running free, whether any rule had been broken — had we quarrelled? had we been late? had we put away the tools? We reported to her faithfully and truthfully, and earned many a minor punishment on our own confessions. We lived in her eye as saints live in the Eye of God. 'Goodness' was all; and goodness consisted of doing what she would approve.

My mother, in girlhood, had been nurtured in High Church piety; and although after marriage she had moved through Frederick Denison Maurice to Driver and the Higher Criticism, I do not think it would ever have occurred to her, while shaping her young family, that for them the ultimate sanctions were not religious ones. We knew, of course, that God wanted us to be good; but I have no recollection of feeling either love for, or fear of, Him. We tried to be good — and we were, I think, good — partly, no doubt, because we knew upon what side our bread was buttered, but chiefly because, since my mother took decent behaviour for granted, we took it for granted too.

There is nothing surprising in that. What is strange, momentous, and of profound metaphysical significance, is that such young creatures, evolved, biologically, from the jelly-fish, should have had such sharp and tender consciences. How did the descendants of the jelly-fish, intent on food, self-protection, and reproduction, come to have in their turn descendants who, well-fed, protected, still sexless, and playing among mellow red-brick walls and ambient scent of mignonette, were to possess that capacity for self-hate as the consequence of a moral judgment which is called Conscience?

Professor Julian Huxley, in his fascinating book *Evolution in Action*, gives the biologists' reply. 'Conscience,' he writes, 'is a piece of mental machinery, constructed by the young child to meet the ambivalent situation that confronts it in its early years. The situation is the co-existence in one person — the mother or some efficient mother-substitute — of authority which is resented, and tender care which is sought and loved. If this situation is absent, as in infants brought up in impersonal institutions, conscience may fail to develop, and the children grow up amoral.'

With all the respect due to one who is a great Humanist as well as Biologist, I am not persuaded that this is a sufficient account of the genesis of Conscience in the young of *Homo Sapiens*. Was it the co-existence of authority and tender care in the mother of Micah, of Amos, and of Isaiah that empowered those massive

pioneers to refashion a fierce and vindictive tribal god
into a God of righteousness and mercy? Was it a self-
constructed piece of mental machinery that produced
the moral fervour of a Socrates, a St. Francis, or even
(for a Biologist can allow no exceptions to a scientific
cause) of a Jesus of Nazareth? What power but Conscience has ever erected and consecrated Revealed
Religion itself? What could the miracles on Sinai
have availed Jehovah, had the Law been 'Thou
shalt kill', 'Thou shalt steal', 'Thou shalt commit
adultery'? What could a Virgin Birth have accomplished, or angels in the sky, or the turning of water
into wine, had the Sermon on the Mount enjoined us
to hate one another? Who would cheer if the Devil
did a miracle?

Our faculty for self-hatred, moral judgments, and
the creation for ourselves of Gods of Goodness, seems a
strange product of an immature animal brain, mech-
anically resolving a conflict in its relations to a pro-
tector-dictator. I am driven to prefer the hypothesis of
an unknown power, working in freedom and interested
in what it has taught us to call 'moral' values, which at
some point in history, possibly as a mere experiment,
took part-control of the psyche of the most highly-
developed animal on this insignificant planet, and made
a man of him.

But if, as I believe, it was the working of this power
in us small animals that gave us, at moments, so much
discomfort, Professor Huxley has every right to ask:
'What about the amoral children at the Institutions?'
He could reasonably go further, and enquire about
amorality, and immorality, at large in this wicked
world. It would seem that a divine spark, to give my

hypothetical power its conventional short title, must, like all other sparks, be fanned. I see no evidence for presupposing a dualistic universe, or 'unknown powers' that, choosing or chosen to work with and through matter, should be exempt from the rules of our physical world. Those rules demand that faculties and functions must be nourished, exercised, and stimulated; failing that, they atrophy.

I have no reason to think that the Workhouse Boys, whom we entertained once a year in hay-cock time, and whose strong smell of corduroys and sweat so offended our sensitive young noses, were amoral; but I am sure that the hair-trigger liveliness of our own consciences owed much to our up-bringing. We lived in almost complete isolation from the corrupting world. The men-servants, the grooms, the game keepers, the gardeners, the woodmen, the carpenters, the workers on the Home Farm, were all delicate-minded men in their dealings with children. 'Master' and his son 'Lad' in the garden — our admired and much-frequented cronies — Dockerell in the pantry, Coachman and Jim in the stables, Mr. Woodhouse at the Carpenters' shop, Mr. Walker, Mr. Plane, and Mr. Billy Owen, must all have had mothers in whom authority and tender care co-existed, or else a divine spark, since their consciences consorted with ours to sharpen, not to blunt, them. They, at any rate, brought us no acquaintanceship with meanness or cynicism. We, on our side, admired their respective skills and their bodily strength, and fell naturally into the Norfolk idiom and sing-song when talking to them. Whether this was always appreciated, I am not sure.

If our consciences were tender, our duties were sometimes tough. Apologising was a dreadful ordeal. To go in cold blood, perhaps twenty-four hours after the offence, to seek out the apologisee; to discover him sitting on the shafts of a wagon with his mates, eating bread and cheese; to have to remind him publicly of an encounter he had forgotten, and to be assured by him that the whole nerve-racking procedure had been quite uncalled for, was discipline indeed.

And there were other duties hardly less stiff. My mother used to attend a weekly Mothers' Meeting in the village. If she was unwell, or had other engagements, she would send us, in turn, to deputise for her. Carrying Louisa Alcott's bulky *Little Women* in a satchel, I would ride across the park, miserably, and tie up my pony at the blacksmith's. Then came the tremulous pause before the drab-coloured cottage door. The light, unemphatic voices of the Norfolk women came to me from behind the geranium-pots on the blistered window-sill. I felt a little sick, but there was no help for it. I lifted the latch and stepped into the musty, fusty, cosy cottage smell, that goes, like apple-sauce to pork, with the ticking of a grandfather-clock. There was a sudden hush, my face burned, and then came the dreaded welcome, the endearments, the surprise at my growth, at my ponymanship, at my likeness to an ugly uncle. It was a relief when the reading began; and it must be considered a feather in Louisa's cap that my love for *Little Women* arose out of, and survived, these terrors.

Is self-consciousness, that worst of spoil-sports, diminished or increased by such early disciplines as these? Cold baths may harden our skins, but I cannot believe that these plunges into misery did anything to toughen the coverings of our shrinking souls. Rather the contrary; as visits to the dentist bring more, and not less, dismay through the accumulation of experience, so shyness grew with the multiplication of occasions. To this day I pause, momentarily, before a door from behind which I hear the clatter and menace of a cock-tail party. All the same, I have not a doubt that, when my mother asked, at the luncheon-table, for a volunteer for the Mothers' Meeting, I eagerly responded, and may well have been selected as a reward for having made the fewest mistakes in the morning's 'dictée'. Can we be sure that the rewards of the older Pharisees were less hard to bear than mine?

It is not to be supposed that my mother deliberately exposed us to these rigours with an eye to our moral characters alone. Her first concern was the Mothers' Meeting; somebody must be there to relieve the Mothers' suspense over Meg's engagement or Beth's decline, and we had all been well-grounded in reading aloud. If we had confessed our trepidations, I have little doubt that the wind would have been tempered to us. Painfully shy herself, she must have sympa-thised with our misgivings. But by training us so inexorably to greet her every proposal with cheerful acquiescence, she cut herself off, unawares, from a know-ledge of our inner thoughts. She was surrounded by 'yes-children', who must have seemed, and did seem, very dear and dutiful to her. I do not say that a habit of putting duty first, by whatever oblique methods first implanted, does not usefully survive into adult life. But I am sure a 'yes-child' does not become a 'yes-man'. The enfranchised worm is apt to turn.

Had our lives been less monastic, we might have lost

our shyness in ordinary easy intercourse with children
or grown-ups from outside the park palings. But such
encounters were rare. Our only near neighbour — and
'near' meant five miles away, at Walsingham Abbey
— was Long Young Red Henry Lee-Warner. He was
still long, but no longer young or even red, for his
great roan beard was speckled with grey. In his youth
he had been a 'card', famous for having drunk up, in
the middle of the morning, the whole of the beer provided for both guests and beaters at a partridge shoot.
In those days partridges were walked up, not driven,
and walked up early in September, before the young
birds became too canny, and too strong on the wing,
for such an approach. An early September day in Norfolk can be very droughty indeed, and the to-and-
froing, to-and-froing of the line through the dry rustle
of swedes is thirsty work. Even so the provision of
great brown earthenware ale-jars, wrapped in red
white-spotted handkerchiefs like the necks of peasants
in an opera, had been nicely calculated to suit the
weather and the party — say four guns and half a dozen
keepers and beaters. They had been dumped in a likely
spot for luncheon, on the north side of a shady bank,
and Long Young Red Henry came upon them when
hunting for a runner. There was a hedge between himself and the party; he was as thirsty as the others but
larger, and he drank up the lot. On another occasion
out shooting, when left of the line, Young Red Henry
saw beyond the clipped hedge his mother's two fat
carriage-horses lazily drawing the Abbey victoria, and
old Mrs. Lee-Warner's red fringe glinting and bobbing
above the dark hedge-hollies. Something long pent-up
in Red Henry's soul burst at last. 'Those fat horses of

D

my mother's have never galloped yet,' he shouted, 'but
by god! they shall today', and as the slow-jogging pair
passed a gateway in the hedge, he let them have it,
right and left, full in the flank. It was at stinging, not
killing range; but gallop they did, all the way to
Fakenham, and it is to be supposed that he found nobody to share the joke when shooting was over, and
Young Henry went home to tea.

I remember old Mrs. Lee-Warner coming to pay
visits, but I must have been young at the time, for only
a very young child could have believed, as I believed,
that her orange-tawny fringe, peeping from below a
black bonnet, had been cut from the rug which lay
before our own drawing-room door — the same rug
upon which I was to be later cajoled into a confession
of my shameful hankerings for the Laureateship. There,
before my eyes, was the very colour, the very texture,
of the rug's familiar, unruly locks; there was nothing
impracticable about snipping off a fragment to lay upon
a little old lady's forehead; and, if a thing can or could
have been done, children do not weigh likelihood
against unlikelihood when the evidence of their own
eyes is before them.

But Henry Lee-Warner himself survived into my
maturer days. We boys would ride over to Walsingham Abbey with a folded note from my mother asking
him to dine and sleep, and while one of us held the
ponies outside the square, blank stuccoed façade, before
which the tall gothic arches of the ancient abbey rose
from a shaven lawn, the other would be led by a silent
butler to where the Squire sat at lunch in his dressing-
gown, with a great leather black-jack at his right hand.
He lunched at four o'clock in the afternoon; and after-

wards strolled across to the church to play the 'cello at
the daily evening-service. Enormously tall and broad,
with high white forehead, red face, and reddish-grey
beard, he had a look of a beneficent King Henry the
Eighth; but only a look, for his blue eyes were wide
open, and not wickedly closed in fatness like King
Hal's. We were not afraid of him, for all the gloom of
the dining-room in which he sat, or that faintly ogreish
habit of lunching at four. And when my mother's
invitation was accepted, we liked to sit up a little later
than usual, to see him come down to dinner in wide
red velvet jacket and knickerbockers, with fluted red
stockings and scarlet morocco slippers. He brought his
'cello with him, and I suppose he played upon it after
dinner; but by then we were in bed, and I do not think
we should have cared much for his playing. We liked
to hear my mother sing, and we liked the accordion on
which Nelly, the second nurse, used to entertain us,
wearing a pair of the footman's trousers, when my
father and mother were safely away at Schwalbach, or
on some rare shooting-visit. But Music, serious music,
meant for us a German band. Our home stood three
miles away from the market-town, and a third of a mile
from the high-road, in turnip-land; a country of
scattered farms and cottages, badly served by railways,
and turning an indifferent face towards strangers. Yet
here, suddenly, on the gravel sweep before the front-
door, two or three times in the year, the German band
would materialise, out of nothing and from nowhere.
We never saw them approaching; we would be, as I
see it now, bending over our wooden desks, or hating
the tapioca on the loathsome flea-bitten grey nursery
dishes, when the sudden blare of brass and wood-wind

lifted our young hearts from dreariness to glory. It is impossible for us today, hearing the word 'German', or seeing it upon the printed page, to divorce the sound or look of it from cruel and sinister associations. But to us these half-dozen men in frogged uniforms, all genuine Germans, all looking like portraits of Bismarck, were heralds of excitement and of a dancing delight. It was an understood thing that even lessons, even dinner might be interrupted; we were given shillings, cocoa, cake and apples to carry to these spectacled angels; and if the music invited us, we jogged up and down to the beat. We were not to know that a man of blood and iron, whom these kindly music-makers so much resembled, had already, in their Fatherland, sown the dragon's teeth.

That Germans could be German even in those days, even in Norfolk, was proved by something that happened at Holkham, the celebrated home of the Coke family, whose great property marched with our small one. A German professor (some latter-day Godfrey Hermann no doubt) arrived, with distinguished credentials, to inspect and collate some rare MSS in the Holkham library. The librarian at that time was the Rev. Alexander Napier, editor of Boswell's *Johnson*, Vicar of Holkham and, like many country clergy in those days, a scholar and a gentleman. It was Napier's task, a pure formality in his own trustful eyes, to sit as monitor while the visitor rustled, noted, and compared with the precious pages spread before him. The day was hot as well as long, and for a short spell after luncheon Napier allowed his eyes to close in a brief, delicious nap. He soon awoke, the rustling and scratching went on; and when the shadows of the great

Holkham ilexes lay long upon the yellowing August grass, the professor finished his work. The valuable books were locked up, intact ; Napier was thanked with guttural effusion, and the visitor drove away. But a few days later Lord Leicester received a letter from the German professor. 'High, well-born Sir, You must your librarian the Reverend Mr. Napier dismiss, for he your so ill-placed trust betrayed in sleeping when on duty. That I did not avail myself of such a not-to-be-looked-for chance of robbing your world-celebrated book-collection, is due not to the watchfulness of Mr. Napier but only to my so German sense of honour.' I am sorry to have to add that, as a chance ear-witness has testified, Mr. Napier banged the study door and Lord Leicester slammed the front door, after this gentleman's letter had been discussed between them at the vicarage. But this must have occurred some years before our time, for we knew this same Lord Leicester, who was the son of the great Coke of Norfolk himself, as an old and rather terrifying bearded figure who lay, wearing a sombrero hat and dark glasses, in a wheeled bed in a corner of the drawing-room. Why he wore his hat in bed I do not know, but we felt it to be un-canny; and I admired my father for his courage in conversing with the Earl, as he was universally called. (We should have been astonished to know that there were other Earls in the world, who went to bed, as I have since learnt, without their hats.)

Holkham was eight miles away on the North coast, and the very name held romance for us. For once a year, in summer, we all packed into a wagonette, known as 'the Holkham carriage', drawn by Baron and Colonel, and were driven slowly along the gritty white Holkham road to picnic on the beach. We were too big any longer to sing:

> Here we go, here we go,
> In the big horses to Jericho,

but not too big to quarrel as to who should sit by Coachman on the box, and watch the fascinating motion of the horses' rounded quarters. I never could make out how it was that a carriage-horse's hind-feet could move so far at each pace with such almost imperceptible movement of his rump. I longed to see this split and fly apart more boldly; to see the stride begin at the root of the tail. Baron and Colonel never seemed to me to be really trying; they were content with a paltry, grudging play of those powerful and muscular behinds.

The romance was not in the beach picnic; that, indeed, was often a disappointment, for at low tide on that shallow coast the sea goes out of sight. The romance was in the first, thrilling glimpse of the sea itself. Xenophon's men crying Thalassa! Thalassa! cannot have been more wild with excitement than were we, screaming in unison, as we stood on the hard blue cushions, 'I see the sea! I see the sea!' An ancient church-tower, covered with ivy, away on our right, was the dark signal that the moment of ecstasy was at hand; but we never could remember the precise spot on the road where a dip in the land would be seen to be barred across by the straight line of the sea-horizon, and there was scuffling and shoving for the glory of the first view. The glimpse was transitory; there was another four miles to the beach; if the tide were out, our first sight of the sea would be our last; and the rest of the long day was anti-climax, only twice relieved as we passed, first, the Giant's Pencil, and, next, the bronze

lion and lioness who kept guard over the forecourt of
Holkham House itself. Nothing to us was the great
avenue of ilex-trees, planted in groups; we were too
busy counting the hares that dotted the rye-grass to
observe or admire the architectural masses, the shim-
mering curves and black shadows of those superb
clumps. It is told that the classic ornaments of Holkham, the statues and the busts, were brought from Italy
in the first half of the eighteenth century packed in ilex-
branches, and that acorns found in the packing-cases
sprouted these lordly aliens. However that may be,
the planting and grouping must have been the work of
a 'Capability' somebody; and yet to children even the
massive ilex-grove around the rather preposterous
obelisk — our cherished 'Giant's Pencil' — was of no
account. We were pleased with the shaggy Scotch
cattle in the park, savouring their bold, spreading horns,
and comparing them resentfully with our father's dull
Red-polls; and we should have liked to look more
closely at the Canada and bar-headed geese upon the
lake. But the lake lay upon the left of the white
carriage-road and if you let your eyes stray to geese
and wild-fowl you would miss the long, satisfying
scrutiny of the noble lions on your right. By the great
house itself we were not impressed. Even adults must
undergo training in proportion and austerity to appre-
ciate the uncompromising severity of Holkham's grey
bricks and reticent fenestration; we children thought it
hideous. We must have seen the gleaming marble hall
and the splendour of the Italianate saloons, for only
through them could we have reached the library, there
to gloat over the Roman mosaic of a lion springing
upon his prey. This, in our eyes, was art indeed, only

equalled, if at all, by the shell-boxes sometimes seen in cottage parlours. But the lion is all I remember of Holkham's glories; and indeed, on our rare visits with my mother to her only Norfolk friend within carriage-reach, 'Georgie' Leicester, it was downstairs we were led by the butler, down into a maze of dark passages, from which we emerged into low, cosy rooms far less ornate and scented than Philip Webb's fantastic draw-ing-room in our own home. And with that mysterious, hatted Earl on a bed in the corner, we were not at ease. The Holkham children were too old for us, although illustrious by repute for being the uncles of grown-up nephews and nieces, and I have no recollection of them. Holkham in those days existed for the sake of partridges; they were the care, the topic, the end-all of its inhabit-ants; and I imagine that its venerable owner's hat would have stood on end could he have foreseen a day when Tom, his eldest grandson, would sit in the long gallery where the classic statues were ranged, and play trios, a Stradivarius tucked under his chin, with Lionel Tertis and a daughter of his own. No, the Stately Homes of England are not for children. Give to them a rare, a distant, an anticipated prospect of the sea.

If Walsingham and Holkham could contribute nothing to our social education, we were not wholly marooned. There were, fortunately for us, the Miss Hoares. The Miss Hoares were grown-up, except one who still had her hair down her back, and they lived six miles away in Colkirk Rectory, but they were entirely delightful. I have forgotten how many Miss Hoares there were; I have forgotten their names — could the youngest have been 'Winnie'? — but I shall never forget their tea-parties, or the new excitement

they brought to the playing of hackneyed games.
'Flags,' 'Witch,' or even simple Hide-and-Seek became,
with the Miss Hoares, and on the lawn or among the
shrubberies of Colkirk, a novel and exhilarating experience. Their strength, their pace, their exuberance, their
daring, their subterfuges — all these made them class
players of our childish games; we learnt from them
what is meant by prowess. How tall they were, and
how their long skirts whirled about us! I have learnt
since that their father, the great bearded Rector, was a
double-blue, the last to row as well as to play cricket
for Oxford, and a natural begetter of 'fierce, athletic
girls'. But the Miss Hoares, although athletic, were
not fierce; they were charmingly good-natured, and
when the games were over and the tea-table spread in
the rectory dining-room, we saw at a glance that the
affair was a 'party'. For there were strawberries and
cream, sure signs of a gala. And the cream was not
that sluggish, semi-solid which crept so reluctantly over
the lip of a silver cream-jug on our mother's tea-table.
This cream was in a milk-jug, and flowed with gener-
osity and abandon over the delectable dark-red and
faint-pink squash which the Miss Hoares encouraged us
to beat up with our forks. I am glad to think that we
had been taught to take off our tam-o'-shanters to the
Miss Hoares as we drove away. We thought it a
finished accomplishment.

Of other children we knew almost nothing. We
enjoyed the companionship of Stanley Fisher, the
bailiff's son, but his father, who afterwards, very properly, hanged himself, lost no chance of warning the
poor boy, in our presence, never to forget that he was
playing with little gentlemen. Although, when learning

the Catechism, my brother had been told, sharply, that 'Master Willoughby John Jones' was not the right answer to 'What is thy name?', we knew perfectly well that we were little gentlemen, and that Coachman had been rebuked for calling my brother 'Willoughby' without the 'Master'; but we knew, too, from singing 'All things bright and beautiful' at the Children's Services, that this was no merit of ours, but God's ordering. And we were acutely embarrassed for Stanley when Mr. Fisher rubbed it in. But Stanley played our games in our own way; and we had our first encounter with the harshness of the outer world when Kenneth and Stephen came to tea.

Kenneth and Stephen were the grandsons of the Vicar of Dunton, a neighbouring hamlet, and must, I think, have already been at a private school. My father, who had an almost pathological scorn for organised games of all sorts, none the less felt, during lucid intervals, that boys destined for Eton should have at least some grounds for disliking cricket as heartily as he disliked it. Kenneth and Stephen were accordingly invited 'to play cricket' with us, and a single wicket was set up on the lawn. Kenneth and Stephen were small, neat, and wiry, in school flannels and caps. We towered above them, with our blue, belted smocks, bare knees, and shock heads. We could not catch, nor field, nor bowl. Our wickets were shattered almost before our bats were lifted. Kenneth and Stephen did not spare us. They had secrets; they had mysterious code-words; they edged up to us threateningly. These little short-haired shrimps made our afternoon a misery. We could have felled them with a blow, but their moral ascendancy was complete. Ulysses derided Polyphemus, who had, in this case, not one eye but no eye, for ball games. I am not sure that on that afternoon my psyche did not suffer a 'trauma' from which it has never recovered. I am still afraid of scratch golfers from White's Club standing together at a bar. I shall always be afraid of them.

Fortunately, before the long afternoon wore away, things took a turn for the better. In these early days we did not look upon riding as an amusement, but as a means of going about. We rode to fetch the fish, or to ask the blacksmith to be ready next day to shoe the big 'oss (since Coachman was of opinion that to Mr. Bird the name 'Egbert' would mean nothing). We had learnt to ride by breaking in, and falling off, Tommy, a wild and wilful Welsh pony. We had acquired firm seats, if heavy hands, but had hurt ourselves a good deal, and got no sympathy at all, since our world, including my mother, held that falling off is the rider's, not the pony's, fault. The day was to come when we were to regard Tommy with pride for his endurance in the hunting field, but in the Kenneth-and-Stephen period we looked upon him much as a child today would think of his bicycle. So when, after tea, Kenneth and Stephen asked if they might have a ride, we saddled Tommy for them with thankfulness for the respite from that beastly cricket-ball, but with no thought that Tommy might avenge us. But avenge us he did. He threw them both, after a short but, to us, delectable exhibition of saddle-holding and mane-clinging. They did not wish to remount. We did so in turn, and galloped about to show our mastery. I cannot help hoping that, to this day, Kenneth and Stephen are afraid of horsey men.

Our boredom with riding, and our indifference towards the ponies, changed overnight after our first day with the harriers. We were sent out improperly dressed, of course, in corduroy Norfolk jackets and red tam-o'-shanters, but at least we had riding-breeches, and our ponies received compliments from the grown-up field which altered our minds towards them. They were henceforth our hunters, to be cherished. But one melancholy incident illustrates the precarious nature of childish elation. It had been our great day; both of us were in at the death with the West Norfolk Foxhounds, rare visitors to our side of the River Wensum; we had been blooded by Charlie Seymour, the Master, and my brother had been given the brush. We rode home in delicious triumph, expecting a welcome fit for heroes. We arrived home at dusk, to be told that my mother was asleep, after a headache, on the drawing-room sofa. The conditions seemed to us perfect. She should have a dramatic, an exhilarating awakening. We crept in noiselessly, and stood, holding our breath, behind her head. Then, with one swift motion, my brother encircled her neck with the furry, odorous object, with its bleeding stump. My mother did not scream, but she was frightened; and being frightened, she was furious. We were dumbfounded. Triumph had turned to disaster and, crushed by my mother's indignation, we could not, for all the Kiplings in the world, treat it as an impostor. The great hunters of that bright morning went upstairs to their tea no more than unhappy little boys.

It may be supposed that it was from living in a ringed fence that I became, and remained, so vulnerable to the sneers, real or apprehended, of the world's Kenneths and Stephens. But at some earlier period my small soul had suffered a more piercing injury which left an ineluctable scar. It was a dreadful experience, for which nobody was to blame. What fell upon me, out of the blue, was nothing less than bereavement, in its sharpest, most widowing form. Our parents had been invited to spend a fortnight with some French acquaintances in a country house near Sedan, and had decided to take my elder brother with them. He and I had never, so far as I can remember, spent a night apart, but in my ignorance of the working of the human heart, I had no forebodings about the coming separation. The day of departure came, and I stood on the gravel and cheerfully waved them away. I then turned back into the house, and in the familiar Entrance Hall, a few minutes ago all happy bustle and excitement, loneliness, a strange and unknown horror, overwhelmed me like a tidal wave. I crawled upstairs to the Blue Dressing-Room, where for some reason I was then sharing with my brother a huge canopied Victorian double bed. On his side of the bed lay his felt land-and-water hat and his leather belt. The sight of these familiar belongings of the Lost One tore me to pieces. I lay on the bed and sobbed, clasping the belt. I had nobody to turn to. I was desolate, bereft, and widowed, without a philosophy and without a comforter. For days I wandered about the gardens and farm, reminded by every sight and scent of lost happiness and of my empty, forlorn situation. There lay his hoe; here was an unaccustomed silence; and in the warm angle of the walls where the hutches stood I dropped slow tears into the rabbits' bran. Many years later, in *La Petite Fadette*, I came upon a description of just such bereavement, and of the anguish of a boyish heart at the loss of a companion. George Sand must also have known the black grief with which even a temporary widowhood can darken the ignorance and defencelessness of childhood.

When I was thirteen, my elder brother died, after a short illness, in the first week of our first summer holidays from Eton. This was a bereavement indeed; but so unaccountable are the workings of immature hearts, that I do not remember taking the shock of real disaster with such hopeless, helpless misery as assailed me on the occasion of our first insignificant separation.

Are children's hearts more insensitive nowadays? Not so many years ago the old wound ached again when I heard, with a pang, of the imminent divorce of two inseparable young cousins. The elder was to go to a private school, leaving the younger behind at home. I made solicitous enquiries, expecting, and dreading, to hear of heartbreak. Nothing of the sort happened. Barnaby was enchanted to be rid of Nicholas; to be the eldest at home; to have the first turn at everything. I was as much relieved as I was astonished.

If children can be vulnerably sensitive, they can also be superficially sentimental. There is an episode in some book — can it have been *Black Beauty?* — which I always thought of as 'The Parting' and about which I day-dreamed. There is a death, or a loss of fortune, I forget which; the consequences were the breaking-up of a household, the selling of the carriages and horses, the dispersion of old servants. Our small bedrooms looked out towards the west, over the stable-yard and the red-tiled roofs of the coach-house and stables. Tall elms were massed behind the mellow bricks; and on summer evenings, as we dawdled over our undressing, and the house-martins swung about the sky, I gazed voluptuously at the golden evening, and thought about 'The Parting' till my eyes were wet with luxurious tears. Goodbye, Dockerell. Goodbye, Coachman. Goodbye, 'Master' and 'Lad'. We were going away. The carriages would be sold. Tommy would be sold. We should never meet again in this world. It was most enjoyable. And when this very thing happened, about the time of my eleventh birthday; when Great-Aunt Rachel left the family money, and the family silver, and the family china, away from her too-trusting husband's nephew, to a relation of her own; when our home was let, the servants dispersed, and the family went abroad in search of economy and cheapness; I said goodbye to Dockerell and Coachman and to Tommy and the rest with cheerful unconcern and inner excitement, for were we not bound for the Lake of Geneva, where there was to be boating and bathing and the Castle of Chillon?

My brother returned from France with a present for me — a slender black walking-stick with an ivory greyhound's head for handle — and an enlarged mind. It was a pleasure to possess a walking-stick with a greyhound's head for a handle, and I never mentioned my sufferings to him or to my mother, nor should I have been listened to with much attention had I done so, so full were they of Mlle Augustine and Mlle Lucie. Mlle Augustine had tended the wounded in her own drawing-room during the battle of Sedan, which had washed about 'La Garenne' like a flood, and she had seen the Emperor, white-faced and dejected, ride slowly past her windows to make his surrender. But Mlle Lucie was a greater heroine. Visiting a strange country-house, and having gone early to bed with a migraine which had prevented a nice inspection of her surroundings, Mlle Lucie awoke to find the moonlight shining upon Satan himself, crouching at the foot of her bed. He had horns and a tail; there could be no question of mistaken identity. Mlle Lucie was a good Protestant, and her character was firm. Reaching out for her travelling-bag, she hurled it at the baleful apparition, crying 'Tiens! Voilà pour toi.' There was a crash, the devil disappeared, and Mlle Lucie turned over and went to sleep. She discovered, next morning, that an immense oil-painting of the 'Temptation' had been used to prop and secure a mattress too large for the bedstead. Her travelling-bag had gone clean through the canvas, leaving a hole where the Tempter had been. Mlle Lucie was not only brave, like so many of her race; she was a better shot than most of her sex.

It was this visit to Sedan, I believe, which led to the coming of Monsieur Georges, who so much enlivened our regular and unexciting routine. My father, who concealed, my mother declared, beneath a heavy moustache an expression of permanent scorn, had a great contempt for a number of things, among them private schools. He believed that there could be no more foolish use of money than to pay large sums in order that small boys should absorb the manners, the vocabulary, the values, the prejudices, and the ideals of other small boys. He disliked cricket, and had a low opinion of most schoolmasters. That my brother and I were to go to Eton was a settled thing, hallowed by tradition; and a soldier uncle, who died prematurely in Burma from not changing his wet clothes after snipe-shooting, had left to my father, in his will, a capital sum sufficient to pay Eton's school bills. But even in those good, easy days some smattering of Latin and Greek, as well as arithmetic, was expected at Eton, even in Third Form; and Third Form was not my father's idea for us. We were to take Remove, like himself. Our governess, my mother, had no Latin or Greek, and very little arithmetic; and after her personal maid, 'Dishea', had shot her bolt teaching us the Rule of Three, and my father himself had found that he had neither the patience, the method, nor the time to teach us Latin and Greek, something had to be done. Fortunately the Vicar of Toftrees, Mr. Owen, was able, and willing, to look after the two classical languages. He was a small, grey, kindly man with the profile, which I am sure did not truly interpret his soul, of a pug-dog; and he and we, with our similar drab, well-trained consciences, got on well enough at the round table in his small dark dining-room. But each morning held its moment of excitement. Toftrees was four miles away; and because it had been decided that my elder sister must also have her chance of a little Latin and Greek, we did not ride over to our lessons, but drove to the vicarage in the cart behind the capricious Tommy. While we were absorbing grammar Tommy was absorbing oats, and when Mr. Owen brought us to the front door to see us off, he was daily alarmed at the sight of his groom-gardener hanging on to the head of a plunging pony, frantic for home. My brother and I took it in turns to take the reins, standing up in the swaying box-cart like a charioteer; my sister, terrified but resigned, crouched on the floor; the groom-gardener leapt clear, and Tommy bolted for home. The sharp turn out of the vicarage drive was the ticklish moment which so

E

appalled Mr. Owen, but after that the charioteer of the day, although unable to moderate Tommy's headlong gallop for the first mile or so, could steer him handily enough, and had leisure to make sure of his stance and his grip before the daily crisis was upon him. This occurred as the road narrowed between the River Wensum on the left hand, and a deep ditch on the right, into which pony and cart had already once been engulfed when lent to some small, despised cousins and their nurse. At this point an enormous collie-dog, believed by us to be a man-eater, was lying in wait for his prey. Out of the white gateway of the farmhouse at Shereford he shot, barking furiously; Tommy and my sister, neither of whom had any capacity for getting accustomed to things, each reacted according to precedent, he increasing his gallop into a panic-stricken bolt, she beseeching the non-charioteer of the day not to provoke the collie with the whip. But the whip was the whole point of the fun; the passenger-brother leant far out of the rocking cart and slashed at the collie with a long lash. Far from intimidating him, this slashing infuriated the collie to ever wilder barkings and leaping; and for half a mile or so, until the collie tired, there was a rattling, swaying, slashing race, all speed and clamour, which was highly exhilarating. Even Coachman's sour looks at the foam-flecked Tommy, panting in the stable-yard, could not damp our risen spirits.

So much for the classics. Mr. Fawcett, the village schoolmaster, was called upon to carry us beyond the Rule of Three, and surprisingly did so in our own schoolroom. Gentle as well as genteel, with steel-rimmed glasses and a scant, pointed beard, Mr. Fawcett

must have walked a mile and a half to teach the little
lady and gentlemen sums — or had safety-bicycles already come into general use? Yes, it must have been
at an earlier date that a man on a bicycle was something to be watched for so long as the windings of the
road allowed, a puzzling and rather absurd apparition;
absurd, because the big front wheel made the little rear
wheel look foolishly inadequate, for all that it so gallantly kept pace with the big one; and puzzling, because
one could not understand how the rider kept his balance
at such a height, astride so thin and spidery a contrap-
tion. But 'pennyfarthings' must have vanished from
the roads almost over-night when the 'safety' was
invented, with its chain and gears; and in no time
there was a Cycling Club at Fakenham, which rode,
wheel to wheel, up the avenue to have tea on the lawn
and to walk round the gardens, while we took turns
to ride an elderly member's tricycle up and down the
terrace. The Club held races, once a year, with a very
sharp turn at the Toll House, where we joined the
crowd that had gathered in the hopes that some of the
competitors, coming down the hill, would capsize into
the hedge. The race was always won, with ten minutes
or more to spare, by the same red-headed young
farmer's son, who 'rode a good stroke', as was said,
until the day when people began to talk, and he disappeared from the Club and the races. The course was
a long one, ten miles or more, with several laps, and ran
past the smart white gates of the farm-house where the
young red-head lived. What people said when they
began to talk was that on the first lap the dirty young
dog had enough lead to enable him to jump off his
machine and exchange it for a lighter, racing machine,

barred by the rules, which lay ready just inside the gates. On the last lap he reversed the 'swap' and finished the race on the legitimate 'roadster'. It needed Mr. Walker, as well as 'Master', to make clear to me what the offence had been, for I admired the young man, and argued that a racing machine must be intended for racing, and that the rules, not the man, must be to blame. But when at length I grasped that my hero had been cheating, I was very much shocked and disillusioned. It was my first experience of a 'grown-up' who could do a wrong and shameful thing; and for many years I associated a certain kind of crinkly red hair with a crooked character. I was also surprised that the crook's sister still appeared, from time to time, in Church. It was not that I thought her brazen, but that for my part I could not, in her shoes, have kept a good countenance in a public place where sin was so freely, and so frequently, alluded to. But safety-bicycles for men were one thing; safety-bicycles for ladies were another thing altogether. There came a day when Daisy Orde, one of our rare links with a more sophisticated world, arrived from the station, to my mother's outspoken dismay, riding one of these most unwomanly machines. Daisy, tall and gallant and graceful, swept round the curve of the carriage-drive, heeling over dangerously, before she dismounted at the door. Her skirts were so audaciously short that you could see her gaitered ankles and, thick as these skirts were, they could not conceal the revelation, necessitated by the action of pedalling, that Daisy's legs were prolonged upwards, above the knee. The cat was out of the bag: Daisy had thighs. My mother loved Daisy dearly, and could go no further than to beg her not to bicycle outside the lodge-gates. How could she guess that in a very few years I should be teaching herself to bicycle upon the shores of Lake Geneva?

Daisy was the most beautiful creature we knew, with a warm, thrilling voice, and an exuberant gaiety. She sang 'Clementine' to a guitar, and made pastel portraits of all the family, singly or in groups, but one. That one was myself. I alone, of the six children, was never asked to sit to Daisy. I had no illusions as to the reason. It was not until I was in Pop at Eton that my face was to be described as 'a jelly-fish with a big toe sticking out of it', but the foundations of that countenance were already laid. Families are plain-spoken, and I knew well enough that eyes sunk deep in chubbiness, and a button for nose, gave me no claims to be painted. Oddly enough, considering how vigorously competitive we were among ourselves, I have no recollection of feeling resentment. It may be that I relished my freedom from the irksome business of sitting, a freedom that brought with it the privilege of watching the pictures grow under Daisy's deft handling of these fascinating chalks. And could there have been a secret, but comforting, consciousness that one born to command had no need of good looks? Sensitive as I was, I received no hurt from being unfavoured with the rest of the family's undoubted comeliness.

I think Daisy must be regarded as having had a share in our education. We had aunts, but none that could convey intimations of the existence of charm in femininity. That the Princesses in our story books were highly desirable rewards for heroes we knew, but could not have answered a plain question as to what these heroes saw in them, beyond their pretty faces. I did not like the female form, and had on several occasions remonstrated with our nursery-maids about their projecting bosoms. 'I would like to cut you down straight,' I told them; and they, embarrassed, replied that it was their shape, which, of course, was just the point. But in Daisy I, at least, became aware of a grace and a graciousness, a timbre in her voice, a beckoning in her merry eye that must be imputed, I knew, to her sex. Men were not like that. When I had complained to my mother about the indignity of having, as my second name, the girlish 'Evelyn', she tactlessly, instead of citing the manly careers of Lord Cromer and Sir Evelyn Wood, emphasised the debt I owed to the care and tenderness of women from my cradle to the present day. I had no wish to be called after the careful and the tender. My elder sister, for all our affection, had not inspired me with any admiration for girls. Conscientious myself, I found her hypersensitive conscience highly irritating. She broke off all our games or ploys to go and look at the clock in the clock-tower, and should we linger beyond her conservative view of a safety margin, she danced about us on thin brown legs, uttering warnings and beseechings that exasperated us. (She danced precisely the same steps, but in silence, when a call of nature was unaccompanied by any opportunity of relief.) The Miss Hoares, of course, were young women, but there was nothing specifically feminine in their robust and whirling approaches and retreats, as pursuers or pursued, on the Colkirk lawns; and it was undoubtedly in Daisy Orde that I first became conscious of some undefined power to attract which plainly belonged to her because she was a lady and not a gentleman.

But these early intimations of the potential value of ladies, important as they were, could not help us to take Remove at Eton, or justify my parents' determination to save us from the imagined futilities of a private school. Accordingly, Mr. Owen and Mr. Fawcett were reinforced by Monsieur Georges, as I have told. It must have been a curious experience for a sensitive, intelligent young Frenchman to be asked to spend his days, for months on end, with a quartet of fiercely Francophobe English children, isolated and countrified. He knew but a few words of English; we had good accents, and were strong on the *participe passé*, but had no vocabulary. Luckily, we were disciplined and docile, if insufferably rude about Agincourt, and Georges' good-nature was inexhaustible. We loved him from the first, and the household were with us. The Pantry had been inclined to suspiciousness for a day or two ; he took such absurdly short steps for a man; they could not like his little round felt hat; and Deloche de Noyelle wasn't a name. But this was quickly changed to 'Mossier Georgy', and in no time he was an established favourite with, I think, a touch of the mascot about him.

Georges broadened our minds. He led us upon highly competitive sketching expeditions, to paint pale water-colours of West Barsham Church against time and against one another. Sucking our brushes, we looked at trees, we saw shadows, for the first time. Apart from possessing a firmer adult hand, Georges knew no more of the technique of painting in water-colour than we did. Our paintings were worthless, but the practice of close observation was not. One curious, and regrettable, side-issue of this artistic adventure was

the spontaneous appearance in our small and primitive
society of mock-modesty. In other pursuits we were
inclined to blow our own trumpets which, admittedly,
stood little chance of being blown by anybody else.
But in Art, unaware of the like hypocrisy of our elders,
we fell into the habit of self-depreciation of our own
accord. Firmly convinced that my drawing was
bolder, my colours more life-like (and imitation was,
for us, the end of Art) than those of the others, I
went from tree-stump to tussock, extolling their messy
little pictures and abusing my own meritorious work.
They returned the compliment. This did not make for
stimulating criticism, and it exposed our valuable young
souls to an insignificant, but genuine, morbid infection.
Still, the balance of advantage was overwhelmingly
with Georges and his sketching parties, and the Frenchman's classic role of civiliser did not end there. Through
our performances of *Le Bourgeois Gentilhomme*, adapted
by Georges to our small capacities, Monsieur Jourdain
became a proverbial hero of the Pantry and the Stables.
Coachman was delighted to hear from us that he, too,
talked in Prose; and Dockerell reflected aloud that
education was a wonderful thing. We had bunches of
ribbons at our knees, and Marquises, too young to act,
sat upon the stage with red heels to their shoes to mark
their rank.

I have already told of how slyly Georges treated our
Francophobia with a dose of Jeanne d'Arc, and how he
aroused our interest in earlier generations. He also
taught us the habit of picking books out of the library
shelves, and used his height and reach to bring down
Travels in the Air, that exhilarating account of early
adventures in balloons. There is a picture in it of a

man clinging to the rigging with both hands while he opens the safety valve with his teeth, and his bearded friend hangs over the edge of the basket in a dead faint, which horrified and delighted us. And it was Georges who pointed out to us the economy of line in Randolph Caldecott's drawings, and gave us, at Christmas, not only a bowdlerised Caran d'Ache, but that entrancing work *Les Mots historiques de la France* with illustrations by Job. Francophobia melted away for ever under the spell of this book's enchantment, and I, for one, can positively date from my acquaintance with it a life-long tenderness for all things French, as well as the capacity to rebuke a smugness in the rare punctualities of an incorrigibly unpunctual family with 'J'ai failli attendre!' Alas for the French, who have every virtue but gratitude. Some years after the First World War, I found, to my joy, in a bookshop at Bayonne, a new edition of *Les Mots historiques* brought up to date. The Great War and the triumph of France over Germany are given much space, and there is a tribute to France's brave allies, the Belgians. Britain and America are nowhere mentioned. It was a shock; but I love the French 'quand même'.

I do not think a private school could have given us anything to compare with Georges' civilised approach to things in general, or with my parents' attitude to things of the mind. Neither was a scholar or thinker, but they read and reflected and talked, often in our hearing, about ideas. They were both at that time influenced by Ruskin, but although we were encouraged to dip into *Sesame and Lilies*, we were satisfied to take Ruskin on trust. All the same, the habit of poking about the library once brought to my brother and

myself a quite undeserved good mark. Our second
half at Eton we were up to Hugh Macnaghten in Lower
Remove. 'Can any boy here name one book by John
Ruskin?' Our arms shot up; nobody else stirred.
'Well?' Out they came, like bullets from a maxim-
gun, Jones major alternating with Jones minor. *Prae-
terita*. 'Good.' *Fors clavigera*. 'Good.' *Arrows of the
Chase*. 'Good.' *Stones of Venice* — and so on, and so
on. We knew the lot. It did us good with Hugh
Macnaghten, but it did us harm with the rest of the
division. Horrid little prigs! With such superficialities
do schoolmasters sometimes have to be content.

Our private reading at this period was much taken
up with the Waverley Novels. These, in order that the
undoubted labour they exact from children should be
sweetened by possession, were given to us, volume by
volume, on our birthdays. It was once my fate to
receive *Peveril of the Peak* in three volumes. I do not
know how grown-up readers react to this work. I
have not tried — and shall not try — to satisfy myself
on that point. I was conscientious, and did not skip a
page, but it was a gruelling ordeal. *The Abbot* and *The
Monastery* had been frivolous stuff by comparison. It
was expected that we should enjoy *The Talisman* and
Ivanhoe, and we were obedient enough to squeeze out
of these books the same sort of dutiful enjoyment that
young fathers derive from the children's hour after tea.
But in all candour, I must confess that *Quentin Durward*
and *Anne of Geierstein* alone gave to me the authentic
joy which it is the sole business of a novel-writer to
purvey. These long hours with Scott induced in me a
life-long suspicion of novelists who describe scenery;
it took a Conrad to persuade me of the profound and

subtle influence that a frame can exert upon a picture.

The days of wooden swords and knighthoods for ourselves were long past, and Scott's romances could not be lived by us, as had been Miss Yonge's. We were pleased all the same, when Archie Campbell (some day to be the Bishop of Glasgow and Galloway, a gay and gallivanting title which exactly fitted him) came charging down the pond at ice-hockey, in the great frost of '95, shouting: 'Hyke a Talbot! Hyke a Beaumont!' to know that our delight in *Quentin Durward* was shared by a fascinating clergyman. Scott, indeed, admitted us to the freemasonry of letters and to the pleasures of literary discussion. Talk about books is the hand-maiden of Reading, and a very agreeable creature she is. Grown-ups who came to tea had forgotten their *Lances of Lynwood*, and were often culpably ignorant of *Jackanapes*, but *Ivanhoe* and *Quentin Durward* were safe bets, and 'Do you like Scott?' was a useful gambit to head off fatuous questions about our rabbits.

But by now we were beginning to ripen, and before I leave childhood for boyhood I am inclined to pause, and to take stock, when the morning dew is beginning to dry from the grass, of the state of this young Norfolk family in the middle of the nineties. What did we know about the world we lived in? What were our pains and pleasures, our affections and emotions?

That this was a world of pre-ordained classes, we never doubted. We felt no sense of patronage when, on Christmas Eve, the cottagers on the estate crowded into the decorated Servants' Hall, each man bringing with him a capacious red-and-white spotted handkerchief. This he unrolled upon a long trestle table, and we children set upon each handkerchief, with our bare

hands, a chunk of raw and bleeding beef, and a packet
of raisins done up in thick purple paper with a piece of
holly stuck into it. My father came in and wished
them all a Merry Christmas, and they wished him the
same, not forgetting the young ladies and gentlemen.
We were not class-conscious, because class was something that was there, like the rest of the phenomenal
world ; moreover, they were all our respected friends,
who simply happened to be 'the poor', and conse-
quently could not expect to dine, like ourselves, off
turkey and plum-pudding. When we visited them in
their homes, we were prone to envy them for their
warmth and cosiness, the shell-boxes, the grandfather clocks, the china dogs upon the mantelpiece,
rather than to compare their cramped dwellings unfavourably with our own. Nobody told us that the
widow Grimmer was bringing up two boys on five
shillings a week from the parish, and lighting in her
grate, from time to time, a piece of brown paper, in
order that she and the children might warm their hands,
for three or four fleeting seconds, when the paper flamed
and roared in the draught of the crooked chimney. Did
my father, the kindest of men, know this? He was
paying his farm-labourers, married men with families,
fourteen shillings a week. But they were lucky, for
they got free milk and butter from Mrs. Olley's dairy.
Did my father know that young Willy Woodhouse,
aged seventeen, who worked in the carpenters' shop,
walked seven miles in the morning, with his tool-bag
on his back, to repair the barn at Kettlestone, and seven
miles home again at night? Old John Basham, the head-
carpenter, drove there in his cart, to keep an eye on
the work. My father swore by old John Basham, and

selected, for old John's tombstone, after much thought, the text: 'The path of the just is as a shining light, that shineth more and more unto the perfect day'. But if John Basham was about to return from Kettlestone half an hour before knocking-off time, not once did it occur to his just mind to wait and give his workmen, or at worst their heavy tools, a lift home in his pony-cart. He rode the path of the just behind his pony, and Sam and young Willy trudged again the seven miles of dusty lanes. Estate carpenters, in those days, received class as something 'given', as we did, together with most of the men on the place. Hard work, thoroughness, and pride in the job were the marks of those men; their endurance, patience, and asceticism were taken for granted by themselves as much as by their employer.

I have learnt since, from a survivor of this generation still living, that their lives were not enviable ones, and that their virtue did not bring its own reward. They suffered. It is all the more astonishing that we children, in constant contact and even companionship with these men, should have heard the name of Joseph Arch so spoken that it had a sinister ring for us. It may be that his support of Mr. Gladstone over Home Rule in the election of 1892 outweighed, except in the mind of Mr. Walker, his doughty services to labouring men. Mr. Walker was a Home-Ruler, and stopped mowing the lawn to argue the case at length with Dockerell, who stood at the garden door and became heated. We ourselves were strong Liberal Unionists, largely because our own candidate, Lord Henry Bentinck, had stayed a couple of nights at our home during the campaign, and had been stoned at Syderstone. (Fifty years later, Henry Bentinck told me of his astonishment at finding a

Norfolk Squire who could talk about books and poetry.) But Arch was elected for the neighbouring constituency; and although my mother rebuked us for calling him an old beast, it was many years before I discovered the truth about this remarkable man. It was as many years again before I overcame my prejudices against 'Old Gladstone'. Why were these remote Norfolk villagers so determined that Ireland should not have Home Rule, and that Mr. Gladstone, for proposing it, and Joseph Arch, for supporting him, were, if not scoundrels, yet next door to it? However that may be, I do not remember hearing one word spoken, by my parents or by the farm labourers whom we so often 'hindered more than we helped' in hay and harvest field, that hinted at the stubborn nineteenth-century contention, not least sharp in East Anglia, over agricultural wages. What did reach us was a talk of low rents, and of rents remitted, and of the losses of the Home Farm. One by one, the laundry was closed, the footman left, and after him the groom; Mr. Basham retired from the garden and was not replaced; my father's riding-horse was sold. We were partly aware, in short, of the economic conditions of the nineties as they touched ourselves; we knew nothing of the cottager's, nothing of the tenant-farmer's distresses.

Our lives were essentially regular, monotonous, and dutiful. True, at a very early age we had been transplanted for six weeks to a house, adorned with stags' heads, in Queen's Gate Terrace, and had attended Miss Brooks' kindergarten near by. With a precocious sense of convention, we resented the fact that our area railings were a bright canary-colour, whereas the rest of the Terrace went in for a dull dark green. Still, we found daily enchantment in the fishmongers' shops in the Gloucester Road; there is something stupendous in the sight of a marble slab flanked by blocks of ice and covered by great, improbable flat-fish. Our sister's finicky retreats from the brave smells of these fish-shops did her sex no good. But beyond a grown-up girl of seven called Maud, who taught me my dance steps, and the story, told by Miss Brooks herself, of how a village cobbler issued once in Rhodes a proclamation that he would be willing to disclose, for a consideration, the way to make in one short day a hundred pairs of shoes, I remember little of the kindergarten. I do recollect that the cobbler's secret was 'to take a hundred pair of boots and cut off all the tops', but that is all. Apart from the delectable fishmongers, London held no joys for us; we hated the dark night-nursery and the narrow water-closet; and although Dockerell took me to Venice at Olympia, where he and I floated in a gondola down a shrunken Grand Canal, my heart hung all upon a sugar-cake rather than upon the cardboard simulacrum of the Rialto. There is such a thing as being too young.

For all London's failure to do so, it might have been expected that a sojourn at Alassio, made for my father's health, would have broadened our budding minds. I do not think Alassio broadened them. We were pulled out of our sleep in the middle of the night, on the journey out, to see the new electric light in the station at Marseilles, but Dockerell slipped on a piece of orange-peel and cut his trousers very badly, and his knee as well, and we were too much frightened and concerned about Dockerell to admire this triumph of science as it deserved. We hated the food, cooked by a bearded man in a high white cap; we were exhausted by my father's favourite climb up the Salita to 'the gap', whence we could see Corsica; and we suffered, with alarm and dismay, from diarrhoea. There was a chrysalis on the pink wall of our loggia, and we looked forward to seeing it turn into some unknown, splendid moth; but one day I attempted, in all friendliness, to stroke it, and it turned into a thick yellowish paste beneath my finger. My horror and disgust, the severity of my scolding and punishment, for long remained with me as the most trenchant association with the name of Alassio. For Italy, as for London, we had been too young. Children have a disappointing habit of taking the wonders of the world for granted, and of grumbling, like elderly clubmen, about the food and the plumbing.

What were the pleasures of our guarded and uneventful lives? Why is Cranmer, seen in retrospect, under a pervasive and unbroken sunshine? I think that, if asked, we should have voted our lives dull. But happiness belongs to the unconscious, and can be absorbed unawares. Children have very acute senses, and they live a couple of feet or so nearer to the earth than do men and women. Where the grown-ups sniffed the new-mown lawn-cuttings from afar, we rolled and burrowed in the heap itself, burying our faces voluptuously in the moist, warm, titillating grass-ends. We smelt the daisies and the dandelions and the clover as we went, without having to bend or pick. The diminutive inhabitants of lawn or hayfield, the ants, the spiders, the grasshoppers and caterpillars, were near, vivid, and familiar. The summer grasses waved at eye-level, and the beards of the barley tickled our cheeks. Our palates told us that bread and butter munched on a hay-cock tastes differently, and better, than bread and butter eaten at the nursery table, just as milk from a silver-gilt tumbler that had been through the Peninsular War tasted differently, and better, than milk from a china mug. I could smell rain on its way many hours before it fell; we could all hear the bats squeak. We loved the smells of stables, of manure, of cows, of sheep, of sliced turnips, of cattle-cake, of the gun-room ; we hated the smell of chicken-houses, dog-kennels, of kid-gloves and carriage-leather. In the gardens, much enclosed by red brick walls or yew hedges, the scents were breast-high for us; but if pinks dominated the square-garden, once you were past the verbena by the green door, beyond the Little Lawn and the bees it was mignonette all the way. And there was a continuous humming, with sudden outbreaks of coo-ing from the fantails. The turf was warm to the back of your hand, as warm as the woodwork of the green-houses when you burst the paint-blisters with your finger-tips. Of all the long winters and east winds of March (save for the long frost of '95) I have no memory; it is always hot, buzzing, summer that I look back upon. Except that even then dusk came, and the bats, and with them an uncontrollable impulse to run at speed, aim-lessly, in any direction, which seized us all like a panic, and was a recognized and awaited enjoyment. We called it, in our pedestrian way, 'feeling runny', but it was in fact a joyous experience; we became, for a quarter of an hour, pure, purposeless energy.

Apart from this sensuous background of the summer days, we had, like all children, our moments of keen and conscious pleasure. Chocolate creams were doled out sparingly; one at bedtime was the rule, never two,

F

never at any other time of the day; but they solaced, effectively, the nightly pang of going upstairs to bed. A more prolonged enjoyment was that of being read aloud to, especially from *Little Men* or *Uncle Remus*. *Uncle Remus* was my father's discovery and province; indeed my mother was quite unable to master the language in which it is written, but my father read it fluently and with enormous gusto, and we rocked and rolled about in ecstasies, like Beetle and his friends in *Stalky & Co.* I have thought of it, ever since, as a work of genius, and it was a disappointment when my own children received it with tepid politeness. But they were little girls, who may not know what's what, or it may be that I, like my mother, could not get my tongue round it. My father was no less successful with the *Jungle Book*; his own enjoyment was as thoroughgoing as ours.

At this point I may as well digress once again in order to describe the impact of my father upon these early days of our uncritical acceptance of things as they seemed. He was still, of a mutually devoted pair, the dominant partner; it was not until we went abroad, and lived in small villas and chalets cheek by jowl with our parents, that we discovered that my mother, and she alone, governed us all, my father included, in things great and small. Tall, handsome, with wavy hair going prematurely grey, with commanding step and emphatic gestures, scornful, sweeping, and admired, my father embodied for us all authority and wisdom. Once the short-lived raids into the schoolroom were done with, we only saw him in hours of relaxation; he never had to solve my mother's problem of retaining our devotion while maintaining a vigilant and continuous discipline. On most days of the week the dog-cart whisked him away after breakfast, to the Board of Guardians, to Petty Sessions, to the County Council, for this period fell into the famous twelve years when my father worked, and worked hard. Having succeeded my grandfather at the age of twenty-seven, after two years at the Bar during which his total earnings amounted to a small silver clock given to him by a Q.C. for whom he devilled, he commenced Squire with an overdraft, mortgages, jointures, a strong sense of duty, and a slight sense of grievance because his younger brother, who became a Bishop, had snatched up my grandfather's gold watch and chain, after the funeral, from under his elder brother's nose. His own father's prolonged reign as Chairman of Quarter Sessions ensured his welcome into county affairs; and his rather lordly manners rescued his personal prestige among his own tenants and retainers from the damage which it might so easily have suffered from his extreme affability and friendliness. When two Cambridge friends hired the partridge-shooting and lodged at the Home Farm, they spoke to the bailiff's wife of their longstanding friendship with her employer. 'Ah well,' said Mrs. Olley, 'Sir Lawrence never were partic'lar who he took up with.' (In after years, when the estate was mine, I could never bring myself to wear my hat in a cottage parlour, and for all the people's kindness to me, my father was always the man for them. He had an air.)

To us, then, he was not only the master of all we surveyed, but the parent who stood for small indulgences, for slight relaxations from the rules, for a drive in the high dog-cart, for a funny book after tea. Not

yet were the days when his many misses out shooting,
the way he bent his knees and puffed out his cheeks
when preparing to hit a lawn-tennis ball, his foozles at
golf, were to sow seeds of doubt about his claims upon
our pride as well as upon our affection. And when he
quoted Tennyson over the first crocus and the drift of
wood-anemones under the chestnut-trees, or read from
the Fourth Gospel, we felt in him a high seriousness, a
faintly discomfiting gravity, which placed him, at times,
beyond our reach, and protected him, for many years
to come, from any questioning, by ourselves, of his
wisdom or judgment.

But I must return to my stock-taking. I think it can
be said that our greatest pleasures, as in the case of all
children, were those of anticipation. Each year before
our fortnight in a lodging-house at Cromer, we saw
ourselves swimming and diving and catching fish with
our hands in a blue translucent sea. Each year Mr.
Maze, the old Cromer fisherman, shook his head and
said 'Cold and choppy' when we knocked at his door
and begged for a swimming lesson. The North Sea is
always cold; in those days it must have been always
choppy. Not once did we bathe at Cromer. It was the
same with birthdays, with Christmas, with going to
Holkham, with picnics, with fishing in the mill-pool.
All these things were enjoyable and enjoyed; but the
thrill, the high adventure into bliss, came before the
event. It was none the worse, as a sauce to life, for
that.

I do not know whether my brothers and sister shared
one intermittently recurring pleasure of my own, because, it was not one that could be acknowledged, even
had we been given to opening our hearts. This private

joy of mine was the absence of our parents. They both
had a tendency to be advised by dear Dr. Kidd to spend
a few weeks at Schwalbach or Mentone. I used to see
them go without anxiety and with genuine relish. It
was not that when the cat was away the mice played
any forbidden games; our well-trained consciences,
and the sober household, saw to that; but there was an
unaccustomed freedom, an easy gait, in our daily doings
which I found most acceptable. It was a feeling like
that of taking off a coat and working in shirt-sleeves.
One could gossip in the pantry, or sit on the kitchen-
table, munching arrowroot biscuits, and tell the maids
things at which, through their lack of book-learning,
they would flatteringly exclaim. Nelly Bayliss, the
second nurse, also felt the lightened atmosphere, and
would bring out her concertina and sing comic songs,
or persuade Coachman to drive us all fifteen miles to
Gayton, to tea with Mrs. Colman. Mrs. Colman may
have been Nelly's aunt, and she was the fattest woman
in the world, and infinitely jolly. The table in Mrs.
Colman's big kitchen had a half-circle cut out of it, so
that Mrs. Colman could approach the 'wittles' more
closely, when sitting at meals. It is true that as regards
her immediate front, her plate was as far off as ever, but
to her right and left the table was more accessible for
this device, since Mrs. Colman, on the horizontal plane,
was not circular but oval. Cream was what Dr. New-
man would have called the 'note' of these teas; cream
that filled a large bowl and was so stiff that a tea-spoon
could be made to stand up in it. It was ladled out onto
scones already crowned with blackberry jam or crab-
apple jelly, and the rule was that you ate till you were
full. At Mrs. Colman's we learnt for the first time the

meaning of repletion, and as we always wore belts (clasped with silver snakes, not wedded eagles) we rose from the table to a general unbelting. Our temperate regimen at home had not prepared us for these physical symptoms; we knew now why Mrs. Colman had to cut bays in her board; and, while we envied her this daily and continuous diet of cream, we also felt that, for our part, we should not be prepared to pay for it with even the smallest cove in our father's mahogany. We had enjoyed a pleasure, but encountered a warning.

Mrs. Colman's out-door privy was also an object of great interest to us. We had been taught to whisper about such places; but here we found a cheerful arrangement of three stalls, so to speak, in a row, graduated in size as if designed for Goldilock's three bears. We were learning that one man's taboo may be another man's sociability.

Our parents' return from Schwalbach or Mentone was greeted with small Union Jacks hanging out of the front windows, and a show of boundless loyalty and enthusiasm. I played my part in these happy reunions with, I hope, every outward sign of devotion, but with mixed inward feelings. My mother never failed to bring us 'surprises', often succulent, and no child was more eager for these than I. But I knew that the shirt-sleeve and slipper life was over; that after liberation must come reconstruction, with its duties and burdens. Was I backward in natural affection? It is hard to tell; we did not compare notes; the convention of our over-riding love for our parents was too absolute for discussion. There had been an occasion, indeed, when my elder sister, who was a kind of embodied Conscience,

confessed to a fear that she had, when smaller, committed the appalling sin of loving 'Dishea', my mother's
maid, with whom my sister shared a bedroom, better
than she loved my mother. And why not? Dishea,
having less responsibility for our morals and being a
natural lover of children, never blamed or scolded; she
was at all times equable and serviceable. The test of
true affection has always seemed to me to be whether
one unfailingly welcomes the company of the loved
one. Without my elder brother's company I could, as
I have told, hardly exist. I enjoyed my parents' company at some times and in given circumstances; for
instance, when the lamps were lighted, the log-fire
blazed, and we clustered round my mother's sofa, in a
drawing-room redolent of cedar-wood and pot-pourri,
to hear *Tales from the Norse* or *Little Men*. But, by and
large, I was happier, because more free, when they were
not there. Freer, not so much from the risk of being
checked or scolded, which was small if one kept to well-
known rules, but from the continual demands for the
outward expression of affection, and for absolute conformity with my parents', which meant my mother's,
views on all questions, big and small. We were each
allowed a favourite flower and a favourite pudding, but,
beyond that, there could only be a wearisome conflict,
certain to end in surrender, if we differed from my
mother in opinions, tastes, or values. To avoid this
conflict, as I had said, we became 'yes-children' and
outwardly conformed; but with the result that, for my
own part, I did not want to hear her step upon the
stairs.

It was over sixty years ago that our childhood
imperceptibly turned into boyhood. It had run its

course under the Eye of the Protestant God, still identified with Jehovah, but more like an English clergyman, who reigned over gentlefolk during the early
nineties; it owed its particular circumstances to the law
and custom of primogeniture; it was spent in close
companionship with labouring men who lived frugally
and cheerfully on the frontiers of destitution, of which
we had no inkling; and it closed with the dismissal of
the footman and the groom, and with the novel sound,
first overheard, then brought into the open by my
father, of the familiar word 'poor' being applied to
ourselves. From being a representative family of the
Norfolk squirearchy, making do somehow with a
butler, house-keeper, footman, cook and kitchenmaid,
three housemaids, two laundry-maids, two nurses, a
coachman and groom, four gardeners, two game-
keepers, two woodmen and two estate carpenters, we
were to become, in a few more years, a family of
exiles, wandering about the Continent, 'poor', rootless,
and, in the eyes of our Norfolk neighbours, decidedly
peculiar. The occasion of this stroke of good fortune,
as it turned out to be, was our Great-Aunt Rachel's
Will; but the cause lay in the parlous condition of
agriculture, in my grandfather's lavishness, in the size
of Victorian families, and in the tyranny of false social
values. We were lucky to have parents who could
wake up, shake themselves, and start afresh.

CHAPTER II

BOYHOOD

OYHOOD proper, I suppose, begins when we cease to make-believe; when the imagination can no longer float us above the solid ground; when we give up acting the characters taken from our story-books; and, more specifically, when we have once tasted the primeval joys of hunting wild animals. I can no longer remember just when it was that I stopped being Ulysses and my elder brother Achilles, and when our younger brothers ran from our elder-tipped arrows as stags, not as Hector and Paris. It may have been on the day that, with a lucky shot, I killed one of my own tumbler-pigeons flying overhead. I was in tears and dismay, but the feat was a notable one, and we were soon exchanging our bows for catapults. I think the gift of my father's acquaintance, Christopher Davey, of his books *Peter Penniless* and *The Swan and her Crew* may have marked the turning point. *Peter Penniless*, the story of an impoverished young gentleman who turned gamekeeper, worked upon us as the re-discovery of the classics worked upon the men of the fifteenth century. Reading it started our Renaissance; forgetting Walter Scott and *The Heroes*, we opened our eyes upon the world about us, and found it abounding in game for our pursuing. There were mice to be trapped in the back passages, mice whose bodies we stuffed into matchboxes, until my mother, coming up to bid us good-night, 'pointed' at one like a setter, and put an end to that. There were rats to be hunted round the cornstacks at the threshing, and rabbits to be chased among the stooks in the harvest field. There were sparrows to be netted in the ivy after dark, or captured under a falling sieve, at the pull of a cord from behind cover. Best of all, there were days with the Harriers and, rarely, with the West Norfolk foxhounds. Taylor, the head keeper, took the place of the gardeners, or of Mr. Plane, the yardman, as our chief crony. We wore corduroys now — Norfolk jackets with belts, and inside pockets for the sparrows. We came indoors for tea with blood and feathers on our hands. My mother did not like killing, but 'vermin' was a word of power before Mr. Aneurin Bevan was born, and she was enough of a country-woman to accept what could not be helped. She was amused at our meals of fried sparrows' eggs, and accepted my brother's honest excuse, when we roasted and ate a blackbird in the Rookery, that he had no idea he could hit so small a target at twenty yards with a catapult. Song-birds were always sacred.

But the earliest and finest taste of what are nowadays called 'blood-sports', fully savoured long before our rat-hunting, catapulting period, was enjoyed by us on shooting days. It was an enchantment on a fine September morning, when the mist had risen and the gossamers twinkled in the yew hedges, to run from breakfast to the stable-yard, and find there, grouped against the mellow bricks under the bright morning sun, keepers and beaters, with the big curly retrievers, and Mr. Arthur Elwes getting out of his dog-cart. The gun-room door was open, and we went in to sniff the delicious odours of gun-powder and oil and leather. Mr. Hipkin, the tall white-bearded head keeper, in velveteen coat and a hard hat, too high in the crown to be called a bowler, used to fill cartridges for his own use with black powder; it lay in open canisters, and a powder-horn hung upon a nail. There was even a ramrod, used for the gardener's muzzle-loader. Mr. Hipkin, as a baby, must have suffered an exceptionally severe conflict between his resentment of his mother's power and his craving for her tenderness, for he had a rare conscience indeed. When he at last retired, and my father made enquiries as to his means, he was surprised to discover that Mr. Hipkin had no savings. 'But your tips, over all these years: a head keeper gets good tips?' 'I never regarded them as mine, Sir Lawrence. They were spent on the game.' For years he had been subsidizing my grandfather and my father. But on this September morning Mr. Hipkin had not retired, but stood tall and straight as the ramrod over the mantelpiece, giving out his operation orders. As for ourselves, we had already drawn lots at the breakfast-table as to who was to walk with Mr. Arthur Elwes, and carry his cartridge bag, for he was the man for us, the gun who never missed. Mr. Francis Smith made more jokes, and was an unrivalled playmate on ordinary days, but not a dead shot by any means; and my father, alas, was a bad one. We minded it sorely, both for him and for ourselves, when he missed with both barrels. My mother told us he had been injured in one eye by a tennis-ball as a boy, but we could see no sign of it ; besides, he got excited, and bent his knees when aiming at a rabbit, cutting an altogether different

figure from that of Mr. Arthur Elwes, all coolness and
precision.

The partridges were walked up in those days, and
we began with a silent stroll across the stubbles, in
extended order, to put the coveys into the roots. It
was long before the days of sugar-beet, but there were
swedes, and white turnips in the headlands, and man-
golds, and a few patches of potatoes, where our short
legs stumbled over the ridge and furrow, hidden under
the blackening leaves. But best of all was a patch of
clover, or of kale, for then the tired birds lay tight, and
rose all round us, even breaking back over our heads,
and Mr. Arthur Elwes dropped his right and left stone
dead, for us to mark. It was all the height of enjoyment;
the suspense as the line rustled forward among the dry
turnip-tops; the sudden whirr and screech of the rising
covey; the bang! bang! and the curl of wispy smoke
from the breeches of the guns as the shooters reloaded.
But our legs grew weary as the September sun grew
hot, and at length we began to lag, and to give up to
the beaters the dead birds we had so proudly carried,
and my father sent us home.

We had no thought of sympathy or pity for the
partridges. Had they been thrushes and blackbirds we
should have been appalled at the slaughter; it was one
of the things we held against the French, that they were
known to shoot the singing-birds. But partridges were
game, destined by their Creator to be shot and eaten;
it was what partridges were for. We knew that a
wounded bird must be despatched as quickly and as
mercifully as possible, although we never learnt to
crack their feathery skulls with our teeth, as the keepers
did; and we were dismayed when a wounded hare

cried out like a child. Nor should we have argued with the Anti-Blood Sport League that, if we gave up shooting partridges, they would speedily become rare, if not extinct, birds. It was simpler, for us, than that. We did not yet know that Nature is red in tooth and claw; but we did know that there are wild birds and animals, which you watch with pleasure and protect if you can; and there is game, which you kill and eat.

I suppose it would be true to say that I have had more enjoyment, a more vivid sense of the delight of living, with every faculty at full stretch, when pursuing and killing birds and beasts, than in any other activity. For sheer exhilaration, joined with the height of aesthetic satisfaction, I have known nothing to compare with deer-stalking. The hard physical grind, the constant exercise of craft and cunning, the breath-taking beauty of the high tops, the subtle and ever-changing colours of Scottish mountains, the solitariness and the silence, combine to exalt the spirit to the summit of happiness. The thrill of fox-hunting is ecstatic, but that has rarely come my way, and the pleasure is more physical than aesthetic. Grouse-shooting ranks high, for the mountains are there again, with their influence sweet as that of the Pleiades; the mountains, too, stand about the lochs, and make memorable many a day's fishing. But there is deep and quiet satisfaction to be had far from any hills; in waiting among the bracken, touched by the mild December sunshine, for the noiseless flit of a woodcock through a glade of ancient thorns, trailing Old Man's Beard; or in hiding among bulrushes, rustling drily, to ambush a flight of teal, or a wisp of driven snipe. Stalking grey-lag geese at dawn on South Uist, or slowly circling a flock of golden plover, in vain hopes of a shot, between Hecla and the green Atlantic, bring the same suspense, the same alertness of observation, the pitting of wits, the triumph or the failure, which are the ingredients of delight; and always and everywhere is the feel of ambient air, of sun or rain or wind, sharp or caressing. For all that tender-hearted town-dwellers write to the papers about blood-sports, blood-thirstiness has no place in these profound satisfactions. So what do I answer to the stags, the foxes, the grouse, the partridges, and the rest of the 'game' whose names are printed, so fatally for them, in my game-book, when I meet them massed in the witness-box on the Day of Judgment? I shall not answer them at all. I shall ask them to vote, on behalf of their kind still upon Earth, as to whether or not sport shall be abolished. There can be no doubt as to how their votes will go, or that they will be unanimous. They will know that, failing sportsmen, there would be no game-keepers, and that without the protection of those watchful and devoted men the game would soon be chivied into extinction, or at best reduced to a bare remnant, living precariously, beset by enemies. The God of nature may be aware of the fall of the sparrow, but He lifts no finger to avert that fall; rather has He given to His other creatures, to His stoats and weasels, rats and hedgehogs, hawks and hoodies, a devouring appetite for raw eggs and young birds which only Man, in corduroys and gaiters, can frustrate. Who watches over the nests? Who traps the vermin? Who guards the fox from the farmer's gun and the deer from the poacher-gangs? Who spreads the corn and the barley in hard weather? Who burns the old stalky heather so that it puts out the young, tender shoots dear to the grouse? The birds and beasts will know well enough; they had easy, pleasant lives while they lasted, and death, which comes to us all, came swiftly before the feebleness of age led to slow and solitary starvation. They will be all for abundance, both of themselves and of their livelihoods, for protection and good cheer; and they will vote 'en bloc' for sport.

For all that, as shooting men grow older, there is, I believe, in most of them a tendency to grow tired of killing. It is the beauty and the fascination of the wild red deer, not the shot through the heart, that counts. The ways of the partridge or of the grouse, studied on the hill and discussed over the port, mean far more than the totals in the game-book. If the game is to survive in numbers, it will be the atavistic hunting instinct in the younger generation that must be relied on to pay for and enforce protection; the grey-heads drift into being amateur field naturalists. But, to satisfy even their milder pursuits, the heather must be burnt, and the stoats hung up, to dry and shrivel and flicker in the breeze, just within the gate of Fox Hill Wood.

To those early days, then, when I trudged proudly with Mr. Arthur Elwes' cartridge bag slung from my shoulder, I owe a taste which, in spite of an inherited incompetence in all forms of killing other than with a rifle, led to some of my finest hours. It was no small endowment, to be — in Mr. G. M. Young's brilliant emendation — 'to the manor born' — a Norfolk manor in the early nineties.

Boyhood brought us, among other gifts, Mr. Jenkins. Mr. Jenkins was just down from Cambridge; he was going to be ordained; he had rowed in his College boat at Henley: he was tall and lean and sunburnt and, as Georges Deloche put it, 'fort comme le diable'. His reign as holiday tutor — we had no holidays, but my parents went abroad that late summer — was short, but it did one thing for us which later meant much to me; it made declared wet-bobs of us. The River Wensum, which bounded the estate where the arable land petered out into Sculthorpe fen, was navigable or not according to the management of the sluices at two water-mills, and there was a boathouse and a punt. Mr. Jenkins was so incredibly muscular, that with no help except our feeble hauling on pulleys of his own devising, he hoisted the punt onto a tumbril, brought it home to the stable-yard, and there added to it a false bow and cut-water, an extra seat and rowlocks. The punt became a rowing boat, and coached by this Henley oarsman, my brother and I were taught the elements of that esoteric art, so simple-looking to the ignorant dry-bob, in which, according to a famous coach, there are twenty-seven separate things to remember as you prepare to cover your blade. In our first summer half at Eton we were in the final of the Lower Boy pulling. I hope we remembered to write to the Rev. Cyril Jenkins.

We had been surprised to hear that he was destined for the Church. Like our own Rector, he had a passion for riding, with billiards as his second choice. He did not appear to read, and he pointed no morals in his pleasant, gossipy talk with us. But he, too, like the Rector, was all godly within, and this was revealed to us, as in the Rector's case, by a sudden, devastating explosion. It happened in the billiard-room. Mr. Jenkins for once missed a sitter, and made a gesture of annoyance. I felt, sympathetically, that such a miss

called for a less restrained comment. 'Why,' I asked
him, 'don't you say dammen b——?' (It is clear from
my pronunciation that 'dammen' was derived from
literary sources, whereas b—— came from Ben, the
cowman's half-witted brother.) The effect of my question on Mr. Jenkins dumbfounded us. He turned
purple; his eyes bulged; he choked and spluttered with
rage. I had no idea that it was possible for a small boy
to sin so deeply, so all but unforgivably, as I had sinned.
Mr. Jenkins was tremendous; he explained, on getting
his second wind, that to utter such words was to touch
the lowest depth of wickedness and infamy. I was
startled and abashed; and for a second time deeply
impressed with the hidden holiness of an apparently
everyday character, as well as with the mysterious and
incalculable nature of God's scale of values. It was
clear that the worst offences, in His sight, could be
committed in all innocence and ignorance. It was fortunate for my peace of mind that I was only sporadically
instructed in ethics by the ordained, or about-to-be-
ordained, Ministers of His Word.

Mr. Jenkins, for all his strength and prowess and
latent saintliness, made one false step with us. Our
dear Georges Deloche was expected on a visit, together
with his lively and entertaining younger brother, André.
They were to arrive by a late train, after our bedtime.
It was Mr. Jenkins' habit to stroll into our bedroom in
the early mornings, before we got up, and to loll across
our beds in his pyjamas while he gossiped. On the
morning after the late arrival of the de Noyelle brothers,
Mr. Jenkins came strutting into our bedroom, with
short, precise steps, and made a stiff, formal little bow.
'Bongjour, Messieurs!' he said. British beef was making

G

fun of the frog-eaters; automatically, on five minutes' acquaintance, by reflex action. I am glad to think that, for all our admiration of Mr Jenkins' sinewy brown arms, brown as the hen's egg we scrambled for at the breakfast table, we were not amused.

I cannot leave Mr. Jenkins without repaying one debt of gratitude. He used to sing to us a comic song, called 'The Cat Came Back', which enchanted us. Thirty, and even forty, years later I used to sing this song, a little out of tune, but 'con brio', to my own children on Sunday evenings at the tea-table. It became a kind of family rite, and was one of those rare occasions upon which a father, generally looked upon, like most modern fathers, with indulgent pity for congenital wrong-headedness, was awarded full marks. 'The Cat Came Back' was a certain and perennial winner.

It was André de Noyelle who encountered a different trait in the British character: that of believing foreigners to be 'capables de tout'. André was staying with another Norfolk family, the Buxtons of Dunston. He had a migraine, and went up to his room to lie down. His hostess, when the shadows lengthened, sent a footman upstairs to ask whether André would like a cup of tea. André had just returned from Germany; half-awake, he imagined himself back there and drowsily murmured 'Nein'. The footman retired, to return in ten minutes with a large tray on which were set out nine cups of tea. Would even the best-trained servant, bred in the belief that his not to reason why, have carried nine cups of tea to that darkened bedroom if an aching, but English, head had been laid upon the pillow? I doubt it. It was simply a case of humouring a member of an unaccountable race, with perhaps a sigh of relief that nine cups of tea and not nine frogs had been asked for.

André threw, for us, a new light upon the French. His brother Georges, infinitely patient in our insular and naïve company, was of a placid and thoughtful disposition. One would never have called him 'our sprightly neighbour, the Gaul'. But André was quick-silver; he sang little drinking-songs and made the noise of water gurgling out of a bottle with enviable virtuosity. He brought with him from the Buxtons, that family of fabulous good looks and charm, their habit of throwing a cricket ball at one another with the pace of a Larwood, and of catching it with the certainty of a Duckworth. We had thought that the French played no manly games. It was we whom André found to be milksops. We could neither throw nor catch. He compared us to the brave Buxton boys unfavourably. He was fair, bronzed, and athletic. We began to understand how Jeanne d'Arc had won her battles.

But if milksops where a flying ball is concerned, we were not physically soft. Our daily preoccupations saw to that. Once the age for imaginative games was past, our main employments, when sport was out of season, were gardening and farming. We took to them, like the majority, not so much from inclination as from economic necessity. Our pocket-money had been six-pence a month from very early times, and was never raised as we grew bigger. Six shillings a year was not a great sum at best; when there are eight birthdays in the family it becomes a tight fit. It is true that after we had presented my father with two enormous spill-holders of brown glazed earthenware, with ears of corn

entwined about their necks, we were given a hint that
my parents preferred home-made gifts to these grand
affairs bought at Mr. Baker's shop. So pen-wipers,
needle-books, and things we could sew or knit or gum,
became the fashion for them. But for each other's
birthdays, an afternoon's shopping was 'de rigueur', and
money had to be found somehow.

We had possessed our separate flower-gardens, by
turn neglected or cultivated with furious energy (as
after reading *Mary's Meadow*), from times immemorial,
but for market-gardening we asked for, and were given,
a larger piece of ground. The boundaries were laid out
with stones; and considering our verbal honesty, and
general conscientiousness, I still wonder how we ever
brought ourselves to commit the 'bassesse' of which
we were guilty. For, noticing one day that a large pear-
tree, which bore good fruit, grew only a few inches
outside the boundary line, we shifted the stones so that
the pear-tree should be ours. As we expected, nobody
seemed to notice or to care; and we looked for a few
extra pears to sell to my father, or to the painters, in
due course. But God noticed, and was not mocked.
On Ash Wednesday we were taken to Church, and
heard, for the first time, the Commination Service.
'Cursed is he that removeth his neighbour's landmark.'
'Amen.' We were appalled. We panted from Church
to the kitchen garden, and restored the line of stones
to its original site; 'fleeing from such vices for which
we had affirmed with our own mouths the curse of
God to be due, and walking more warily in those
dangerous days'. The painters, who seem, in retrospect, to have been eternally crawling over the long
line of greenhouses, were our best customers, for peas

and broad beans and potatoes, and for bantams' eggs. They paid ninepence a dozen for these, and one and sixpence for a cockerel. I am sure my mother had no idea that her dear little boys used to kill the cockerels with their own hands, in the little wood by the stables, in the right professional manner. We strung the bird up by its legs upon a tree, and slit the roof of its mouth with a pen-knife, so that it should bleed slowly to death, ensuring clean white meat for the painters' Sunday dinner. The cockerels showed no sign of pain or even discomfort, but drooped inertly with placid eyes, till a film closed them for good and a last flutter signalled death. Only a long black streak on the tree remained to tell of our lethal work, done without pleasure or disgust, as a matter of necessary business.

But a sieve full of beans, or a quarter of a bushel of potatoes, bring in a matter of pence only; and as the 'res angusta domi' pressed upon us, we decided to take to farming. We hired about an eighth of an acre on the Home Farm, paying the market rent for it. We were subsidised, because my father did the ploughing and harrowing, but we sowed the oats, broadcasting by hand, and reaped with the big shears used for trimming the yew hedges. And, in due rotation, we perseveringly planted out the white turnips. We paid the rent on Michaelmas day, after waiting our turn outside the Justice-room door with the other small-holders and cottage-tenants, and resenting their patronising chaff. We also fattened a pig. Mr. Sewter, from whom we bought it, offended us mortally by sending in his account: 'To one nice little pig, 10s.' That was no way for a dealer to render his bill to a farmer. We paid ten shillings for feeding-stuffs, and sold the pig for thirty shillings, making a handsome profit. But the big money came from two turkeys we managed to rear, out of a clutch of five eggs sat upon by a bantam hen. Three died suddenly, and in company, when they were half-grown; there were no marks upon them, but it happened at night and the gardener told us that turkeys had the gift of dying of fright. This opinion relieved us of any responsibility for mismanagement, and was gratefully accepted. The two survivors were sold to Mr. Jack Smith, the head of Smith, Elder and Company, the publishers. One weighed 17 lbs. I have forgotten the price, but it was paid partly in gold, and enriched us. The great birds had been subject to their diminutive bantam-foster-mother to the last, and we had feared that she would pine for them; but she seemed as cheerful as usual on Christmas Eve. Farming is a heartless business for all concerned.

Whether farming is a better occupation for small boys than playing cricket under the eye of a games master at a private school, I cannot tell; but it hardens the hands and the heart and makes countrymen of them for life. I have never wished to farm again, even when I owned the land; but I have a natural sympathy with growing crops, and it is their indolent and passive part in the business, not that of the laborious and harassed farmer, which appeals to me. I like to lean upon a gate and watch things grow, and have no longing to sit upon the tractor. But I shall always be at home in a farmyard, and I can appraise the young stock, and be glad to see the dew upon their noses, without a thought of envy for their master. After all, we only went into farming to make money, and having made as much as I needed, I am content to let others have their turn.

But towards the soil, and the working of it, I can never
be a stranger, or unconcerned.

We were not alone in being pressed for money, and
by this time our lives of busy seclusion as little Masters
and Misses were drawing to their close. It was almost
as if Cranmer itself had its forebodings; there were
portents, and visible cracks in the fabric of our familiar
backcloth. If there is one thing more than another
which can recall to me, in one swift, sufficient stroke,
Cranmer as it then was, it is the noise of rooks; not the
desultory cawings of March, round and about the high
nests, for our Rookery was some way from the house;
but the grand confused clamour, with the jackdaws'
lighter clacking as descant, of the evening assembly.
This took place, not over the elms in the Rookery, but
above the house itself, and the lawn spread before it, and
over the old oaks in the avenue, from which the jackdaws flew up to join in the parade. The sky was black
with the interweaving cohorts, purposefully purposeless, and the hubbub was tremendous. Was it discussion? It sounded at times like discussion, vehement
enough, with sudden outbursts of cheers or derision,
then suddenly diminished into general conversation,
amicable and gossipy, with a dropping exchange of
casual afterthoughts. But whatever the rooks were at,
their familiar cawing belonged to us; we, and the old
brick house itself, had our rights in it, and when it
ceased, it must surely have been a sign. For cease it did,
and mysteriously. We shall never know what rooks
know; but in the spring of '94 they abandoned the old
rookery and their tall elms, and migrated half a mile
to the Old Square Wood, building uncomfortably in
beeches and sycamore and ash which had shot up there,

unforested, into gawky poles of unnatural habit. A
year later, in the March of '95, came the great gale.
Over seven hundred trees fell in the park and belts, and
the old Rookery was wiped out. Not an elm remained
standing. It was the nesting season, and the rooks in
their unpretentious and pliant hotels suffered only
moderate casualties. All the same, they went off that
year for good, nobody knows whither; and Cranmer
has never had rooks again.

We watched the trees falling only from the windows, for the air was full of flying slates and chimney-
pots, and we were forbidden to experiment, as we
longed to do, with the effect of such a wind upon
ourselves. We saw a strip of lead, more than a yard of
ponderous metal, fly upwards in the air like an autumn
leaf, to fall and bury itself in the lawn. We saw the
Six Sisters, a group of co-equal silver fir, collapse
together like corn before a scythe. We were greatly
excited. As the tale of ruin grew, we were humiliated
to learn by how much our poor seven hundred had
been exceeded by the falls on the larger and more
closely-timbered properties around us. We shared the
shame of smaller nations, whose losses in Korea are
deemed inadequate. We should have liked to have
lost two thousand trees. The windfall was no windfall
to my father, already enslaved to an overdraft, for the
glut knocked the bottom out of the timber market.
But it brought us nothing but profit; still blind to form,
if not to scent or colour, we found a great beech-tree
prone far more exciting than in the days of its spreading
majesty. The enormous mushroom of matted roots
and earth, upstanding like a plate on edge at the side
of the crater whence it was torn, was something delight-

fully novel, revealing, and climbable. It was amusing
to balance along the smooth grey length of the horizontal trunk, and to clamber, familiarly, among branches
and twigs which had lately been accessible to none but
birds and squirrels. And where a whole wood had been
uprooted, as in the case of the Rookery, there were
lofty and intricate entanglements, as high as a house,
often impenetrable, always inviting, which called,
irresistibly, to our primeval arboreal instincts. We
found them, to our surprise, harbouring a disunited
group of shy and resentful cats.

So the sky was empty of rooks, and the park and
woods disfigured and criss-crossed with the great
furrows made by the fallen trees, dragged in chains by
the steaming teams of shire-horses, hairy-heeled and
enormous. It had been fun to watch the men barking
the trees, ripping off the bark with a crackling noise
which gave one the same sensuous thrill as is to be got
by walking upon horse-chestnut pods or upon cockle-
shells when the sand is firm. The bark was piled for
the tanneries; but the trees were laid in groups at
accessible points, and sold by auction. The auctioneer
wore a bowler hat, and knocked down the lots by
whacking the smooth butts with a hammer. Although
my father was to get the money for them, he said it
was ruinous, and showed no pleasure.

Perhaps Great-Aunt Rachel had already died, and
her Will been read? She was Rachel Gurney, and had
married my great-uncle, who held the family living for
thirty years, and ruled the parish as only the Squire's
brother could. He used a carriage and pair for visiting
the cottages, and such was his influence that when, in
jest, he said to a parishioner: 'I should like to have the

burying of you, George,' George went home, to d his
wife, refused his food, and died in three days.   Great-
Aunt Rachel used to drive a pair of smart ponies in a
low carriage, with a little seat behind for the groom.
He wore a top-hat with a cockade, and was very small
and old, but it was Aunt Rachel's whim, when Billy
Skipper alighted to open a gate, not to wait for him
to climb up again upon his exiguous perch, but to let
him sprint after the carriage and scramble up as best
he could.

She was a woman of character, an antiquarian and
genealogist who could paint birds and butterflies and
wrote a life of the Princess Charlotte.   My great-uncle
trusted her, and left all he possessed to her absolutely,
knowing that she, being childless, would leave it back
to her eldest nephew.   But he knew wrong, as our
nurses used to say: and it was a Gurney relation of hers
who had the laugh on my father.   And her little game
became, as I have told, the occasion of our going.

My great-uncle, whom I remember but dimly, was
a handsome, indolent man who never preached on
Christmas day, telling his congregation that he knew
they were all agog to get home to their Christmas
dinners.   He was mildly musical, and would call out
'Rachel, my love!' to his wife at the Church organ,
bidding her play faster or more slowly, for he had his
own ideas how the hymn-tunes should be played, and
she, it seems, had hers.   He had been a figure in the
parish; and when, sixty years after his death, an elderly
lady who had known him as a child remarked to an
old gaffer at his gate that she supposed he could scarcely
remember the old Rector, he replied, with some heat,
'Of course oi moind him: he doyed of a Tuesda''.

Of many of us, perhaps, still less will be remembered.

So 'the parting', of which I had day-dreamed on summer evenings long ago, came in very truth. Cranmer was let and the household dispersed; only the faithful Lizzie Lee, my small sister's nurse, came abroad with us, and Amy the cook. Lizzie Lee, for all her virtues, did not stay with us long, for in the close quarters of our life in villas and chalets her profile, which was that of a teapot, got upon my father's nerves, and as she was unable to alter it, she had to find another situation. Life can be hard for the chinless.

We shed no tears at our going. Children are elastic, and love novelty, and our parents sensibly built up, for our minds to dwell on, a most delectable picture of the Lake of Geneva. For Clarens was our first stopping-place. We hired a 'coquette villa', one of a group called the Villas Dubochet, of fantastic architecture, with small round turrets, capped and hatted with coloured tiles. A little island with weeping willows lay close off-shore, and there our charmed eyes rested, rather than upon the Dent du Midi, or the mountains across the lake. We had seen the snow mountains of Corsica as fledglings, and had even looked at Whymper's book in the Library, but it surprises me now to remember how we took the landscape for granted, and how little we were stirred by heights and the glimpse of eternal snow. We enjoyed laughing at Lizzie Lee, who, brought up to gaze across the level turnip-fields of West Norfolk, opined, in answer to our questions, that the mountains on the far shore were about twelve feet high, and that the houses of St. Gingolph and Bouveret were white pebbles at the water's edge. But I remember no lift of the heart, such as mountains, and even hills, have always given me in after years; we wanted to swim, and to go in a boat, and on our very first day we met an American boy who put scenery right out of our heads.

He was riding a bicycle round and about a disused tennis-court, which was common to the inhabitants of the Villas Dubochet, and doing simple tricks, such as riding with folded arms. He must have been about fifteen, with a complexion like putty, and a white linen cap with a peak. He was cocksure, and rather ill-conditioned, using to us smaller boys at our first encounter some vulgar terms, which were new to us, for parts of our bodies and functions; perhaps they had been lately new to him. But he was good-natured, and seeing our eager and envious faces, at once offered to teach us to ride his bicycle. We, who took ponies as a matter of course, had long pined for bicycles, much as children today, who are born knowing how to bicycle, pine for ponies. By the end of the morning we could wobble round the tennis-court, and before the day was over, our parents had been summoned to watch us riding up and down the lake-side boulevard. We were in ecstasies. If this was life 'abroad', then abroad was the place for us. In no time my father had been persuaded to hire a small lady's Rudge-Whitworth from the Café Simplon, and we took it in turns to ride to and fro upon the serpentine road which wound among those improbable villas. And it did not end there. My father himself caught the infection, and was soon riding a 'high-frame' Singer, also hired, and within a week we boys were supporting my mother, one on each side of the Rudge-Whitworth, and bidding her turn her front wheel in whatever direction she listed. My mother did not hire a bicycle that summer, but there was no more talk of unwomanliness, and by the winter she owned her own Peugeot.

Singer, Rudge-Whitworth, Peugeot — only from the middle nineties could the names of bicycle-makers be remembered. But for a few years people bandied these names about as they now bandy the names of motor-cars, each championing his own, as we do our doctors and dentists, because he had known no other.

We soon learnt to swim, with red bladders floating at our shoulder-blades, in the shallow inlet where the lake-water was warm and encouraging, unlike our bitter Cromer sea; but our parents had not brought us to Switzerland only to swim. Expeditions were made to Les Avants, to see the great fields of narcissus, and to the Dent de Jaman and the Rochers de Naye, to show us splendours and to let them do their work upon us. I believe the splendour did do something to the 'unconscious' in us (for all it had not then been heard of), but as concerns our conscious minds, I am sorry to say that it was the Sirop de Groseilles that made our day. We did not much like going uphill and got tired hunting for Alpine flowers with which to fill the green tin cases slung about our shoulders, and the thick V-shaped glasses of Sirop de Groseilles diluted with glacial water, which were given to us as our reward at the top, were looked forward to greedily and remembered lovingly. My father was a bit of a botanist, and encouraged us to collect and examine the dwarf wild-flowers, and did his best to make us remember their names and families; but there were so many called 'one of the milkworts' that even my mother hinted that he might not be infallible. Milkworts, she felt with us, should have some family resemblance to one another, however faint

and elusive. We did not become botanists, to my last-
ing adult regret; for myself, birds took the place of
flowers, and have given me perennial pleasure and
interest. It is surprising that my father, so fond of trees
and flowers, should have been bird-blind. He was not
far removed, in this respect, from Mr. A. J. Balfour,
who came down to breakfast at Whittingehame with
the news that there was a little bird in his bedroom.
'What kind of bird, Nunky?' asked one of his nieces.
The celebrated eyebrows went up: 'What do you
mean by "kind"? It was just an average little bird.'
My father, however, did recognise species: to this day
he believes that there is a bird called the 'Hay-bird',
which visits Norfolk in June and makes its nest in the
sides of hay-stacks. It must be one of those rare birds
which my own children, in due course, used to discover
on their walks. Knowing my hobby, they would
return, flushed and eager, and describe, in minutely
observed detail, a bird that never was on sea or land.

In a French-speaking country, my mother rightly
felt that it was time for us to practise conversation, as
well as reading and writing, with a native: and fortunately Mlle Scheiterburg was available and willing.
Mlle Scheiterburg belonged to an ancient Vaudois
family; if Blonay was not her ancestral home, it had
been in the Blonay class, but she was poor, and shared
English friends with my mother, and, what was best,
liked and could be companionable with children. She
even took charge of us when my parents went off to
search for a mountain chalet, as a refuge from the
summer heats. But young minds, unlike sundials, do
not record only sunshiny hours, which they take for
granted. The two marks made by Mlle Scheiterburg

upon memory's tablets, marks which alone time has
not erased, are that she had not been born to teach
or to look after children, and that she had lately lost
her mother. I can only suppose that she took pains
to impress upon us her Blonay-like provenance, but,
touching her lost mother, I vividly recollect the deep
and gusty sighs which punctuated both lessons and
meal-times. This sighing disturbed us a good deal; we
were sorry for her and sorrier for ourselves: and I am
ashamed to say that we had a sneaking sympathy with
some Isabel, the English friend shared with my mother,
about whom Mlle Scheiterburg would never feel the
same. For Isabel, in a moment of compassion, had
invited Mlle Scheiterburg to pay her a visit of some
weeks, soon after the sad bereavement; but, before the
visit ended, had forgotten herself, and had, on more
than one occasion, laughed and joked with her brothers
in Mlle Scheiterburg's presence. We thought it rather
hard on Isabel that for these moments of faltering in
her self-imposed task she should never be felt the same
about.

Had Mlle Scheiterburg not so handily popped out
of her top drawer, heavily veiled in crepe, to chatter
with us between sighs, we should have learnt little con-
versational French; for, except for the man-parlour-
maid Auguste, we made no Swiss friends at Clarens.
Auguste was a big, fair, blue-eyed giant in an apron,
to whom we boys became greatly attached, and with
whom we fished for perch from the pier when his work
was done. We learnt from him a few angling terms,
but he was not a conversationalist, and his pronunciation differed from that of Mlle Scheiterburg and that
of my mother. Even my father, who loved to talk to

strangers, and was eager to exchange thoughts with intelligent foreigners, found himself exchanging rather threadbare ideas with an American colonel much of the time. We rather despised the colonel for calling the Café Simplon, where he also hired his bicycle, the caffy samplong; we knew so much better than that. As for our hosts, the people of Vaud, we took a great dislike to them. They shouted at us when we crossed their little meadows; we were warned off all the most exciting footpaths; and on one occasion, when we jumped a ditch to pick yet another species of milkwort, a farmer ran at us, waving a pitchfork, and bullied us into paying him five francs. It was our all; we protested that we should be bled white, but he pointed to a notice board — 'Défense d'entrer: Amende 5 francs', and that looked to us like the law, which we supposed must be obeyed. We went home furious, and were not comforted by my father's opinion that we had been little fools to pay up.

Knowing nothing of Burke, we thereupon indicted a nation, and did not relent until we had exchanged trim, sullen, Protestant Vaud for dirty, friendly, Catholic Valais. And I do not think my recollection is at fault. We met no friendliness on our walks abroad; the shop-keepers were gruff and grudging. When our parents' friends, the Gurneys of Keswick Hall, were at Montreux, and took us up the hills one Sunday morning to an out-door Lutheran service, I did not like the looks or the drab clothes of my fellow-worshippers as they stood to pray. 'They seem very devout,' said Mr. John Henry Gurney. 'Devout' was a word I had been uncertain about; now I knew. It meant cross-looking.

In justice to an admirable race I must add that when

I revisited the Canton of Vaud forty years later, I found
the people of Lausanne courteous, helpful and forth-
coming. But by that time devoutness had, perhaps,
gone out of fashion.

My parents had found a summer chalet at the Mayens
de Sion, a scattered group of chalets and one small
wooden hotel, high above Sion on the south side of the
Rhône Valley. Again, they cleverly built up for us
expectations of fresh delights, of cowbells and yodelling
and alpenrose, to wean us from the uncloying joys of
the warm lake-water. But before we ourselves became
those 'enfants de la montagne' of whom Mlle Scheiterburg had taught us to sing, we had one memorable
initiation at Geneva. We went to our first play. It
was Labiche's *Le Voyage de Monsieur Perrichon*, that
amusing parable illustrating the undeniable truth that
we are less grateful to those who save us than to those
we save. We had read the play with Georges, and had
no trouble in following it, but we should have liked
any play on that occasion, seen from those plush chairs,
in that gilded and overhanging box. I have long since
lost all sense of, or taste for, the glamour of Empires
and Alhambras and Café Royals, which never ceased
to enchant and to inspire a Degas, a Manet, or a Sickert.
But on that night the curves and the curlicues, the
pilasters and the cornices, and all those festive protuber-
ances that distinguish a theatre or opera house from any
other place of assembly, had their full effects upon my
inexperience. The revelation of that evening, however,
was for me neither the humours of M. Perrichon nor
the charm of theatre-baroque. It was Gilda's bosom.
For, curiously, there was a double bill for our enter-
tainment, M. Perrichon being followed by *Rigoletto*. I

H

had seen plenty of ladies in low dresses, including Daisy Orde; but never before had my eye been caught and held by a silky sheen, as of white satin, such as rose and fell with the breathing of this exquisite creature. Could this indeed be skin, I wondered, that shimmered and glistened so, or was it some subtle material, cunningly fitted? I had young eyes; I could not be deceived: this was indeed a woman's own skin; and I carried with me from that memorable evening a new understanding of what the heroes of our story-books may have seen in their heroines. If all Princesses and beautiful maidens had chests like Gilda's, their price in hazards and miseries may not have been too high after all. I did not discuss Gilda's chest (as I thought of it) with any-body, not even with my brother. This was not delicacy about the feminine form, but shyness, and perhaps a little slyness, about my secret possessions. For in some indefinable way I had a conviction that the tactile value (as Mr. Berenson might have put it) of Gilda's chest was for me alone. I have often, in maturer years, had the same most acceptable impression of being the sole possessor of a sudden beauty, whether found in a woman, a mountain, or a William and Mary façade.

When the hot weather came, we migrated, our heads full of marmots and edelweiss, to the Mayens de Sion. It was exciting to be met at Sion railway station, not by cabs or an omnibus, but by Monsieur Pitlou and his nine mules. M. Pitlou shook hands all round with the courtesy of the Valais, where the saints, and not Calvin, ruled; and, with his boys, deftly strapped the heavy leather trunks and portmanteaus of the nineties upon the mules' backs. 'And how do we get to the Chalet?'

'You,' said M. Pitlou, 'will walk.' And walk we did, to our great misery and disillusionment. Once the dirty white Rhône was crossed, the zig-zag path was steep and stony; we struggled up for hours; we were hotter, and thirstier, and more tired than we had ever been before, and we already began to pine for the level shores and cool waters of Clarens. There were no marmots and no edelweiss; not a yodel could be heard, not a chamois was in sight.

The Chalet Blanchaud was a further disappointment. We had seen many pictures of chalets, and had even possessed an exquisitely carved model of a chalet in miniature, all gables and overhanging eaves and elaborately ornate balconies. This one was a simple rectangular box, without eaves or balcony, erected, I suppose, by the local carpenter. A narrow passage ran from the front door to the highly embarrassing earth-closet; smaller boxes, square and lined with pitch-pine, flanked the dark central corridor. There were no pictures on the walls. There was no hot water in the taps. After the turrets and gables and balconies and ingles of our fascinating Villa Dubochet we felt badly let down.

The child is not the father of the man. During most of my life I have loved going up and down hill, and associate that kind of exercise with my happiest hours. But at the Mayens, although this distasteful deal box stood upon a small level shelf, all ways led uphill or downhill; there was no profit in choosing the easier downhill way, since the way back must be, irremediably, uphill. It was an aspect of the mountains that, somehow, had not occurred to us. We disliked it heartily.

My parents handled the situation with skill. Presumably abhorring the earth-closet as much as we did, they found pressing reasons for a flying visit to England. And they replaced the marmots and edelweiss in our heads with La Bataille des Vaches. It seemed that upon a day in the near future all the cows from the villages below us would be assembled for the summer grazing on the high alps above us. And a cow-fight would take place between last year's Reine des Vaches, an elderly dowager who wore the master-bell round her neck and went first in to the milking and first out to the pastures, and the younger challengers for her position of primacy. It promised more than well. A second, and younger, Mlle Scheiterburg, of still older lineage, was found to take charge of us. There was no vagueness about Mlle Cécile de L.'s background. Her home, in the middle of sweltering Sion, was encrusted with coats of arms. The cool, dark, spacious rooms were hung with tapestries, and crowded with tall presses, polished and black. The chairs were not to be sat upon. The Sirop de Groseilles was served in high, thin goblets with twisted stems.

When the day came, Mlle de L.'s brothers and sisters and cousins arrived early at the Chalet, laden with knapsacks, and the whole party set off for the Crêtes de Thyon. For once we forgot the steepness. The brothers and cousins yodelled as they went, and sang songs about the joy of being a mountaineer. I asked one cousin how old he was. 'L'âge de Jésus-Christ.' I was a little shocked. So Christ, too, had birthdays, like us. But the cousin's yodelling, his gaiety, his friendliness, enabled him to live it down. It was our first experience of continental high spirits, of spontaneous frolic. Not

till I went up to Balliol did I rediscover the mood, and
the singing that went with it. Could it, even there,
have been caught from the continental Belloc?

It was well for us that we were in such exhilarating
company, for the Battle of the Cows was a sad failure.
The old Queen, a long lean black animal with acute,
forward-bending horns, was there with her great bell.
But she grazed peacefully all day, and her challengers,
whatever their intentions may have been in the valley,
had thought better of them when they saw those horns,
or perhaps it was the new grass of the alps. Whatever
their thoughts, they also grazed peacefully. There were
desultory combats between young bulls, fought, like
those in Shakespeare's plays, 'in another part of the
battlefield.' But it was a pushing with foreheads; there
was no savagery, no goring, no gore. By now the
cousins were unpacking their knapsacks, and we were
being introduced to pâté de foie gras, to thin mottled
slices of sausage, and to an ambrosial cake called 'mille
feuilles'. A herdsman brought bowls of stiff cream
from a dark, cavernous cow-shed, and we loosened our
belts as we had loosened them, in those distant days,
after tea with Mrs. Colman. Food is a great comforter,
whatever the age of the eater, and we soon forgot the
backsliding of the challengers for queenship. They
were, after all, only doing what we were doing: enjoy-
ing a meal on a mountain. And we enjoyed ours,
literally, to the full.

It was a red-letter day in spite of the pacifist cows,
for we were high enough to pick alpenrose, and to see
the peaks of the Oberland. We did not want to climb
them, our legs that day were too tired for such ambition;
and it was not until a later occasion of a night spent in

the hotel at Arolla when we saw real climbers returning, with sun-peeled faces and coils of rope, that we began to crawl over the erratic blocks that lay here and there upon the lawn-like alps. Later still we were taken to Zermatt and the Riffelhaus, and saw chamois through a great telescope from the hotel terrace. But so myopic is the eye of extreme youth, that my sharpest memory of that hotel is not the prodigious Matterhorn, but a bearded guest singing, in the salon after dinner, about an old horse that died. Mountains, like stately homes, are wasted on the young.

But the principal cause of our unease that summer at Les Mayens was our fear of thunder-storms. These rolled about us, and with heavier menace below us, almost nightly. Oppression came upon us with the approach of night; and in our hot pitch-pine boxes, with uncurtained windows, we lay and quaked as the thunder cracked and reverberated. It was terrifying to see forked lightning not in the sky, but below us in the valley. The hotel, a few hundred yards away, was struck. When would it be our turn? There were no fire-irons to put under the mattress, as we had seen our nurses do when a rare Norfolk tempest had crashed and passed away at Cranmer. No such comforting pro-phylactic action could be taken on the mountainside. The clamour was insistent and continuous. It got us down.

The Chalet was also the scene of a very different sort of depression. An old Cambridge friend of my father's, Mr. Francis Smith, came to pay us a visit. He was an immense favourite with us. He made splendid jokes. He joined us enthusiastically in our study of ants, a novel preoccupation which engrossed us for many

hours a day. He admired our model water-wheels.
He discussed harmlessly, with my parents, the merits of
Mrs. Humphry Ward's latest novel, *Marcella*. Then,
unexpectedly, the blow fell. He asked my father how
we were getting on with our Latin. My father rashly
suggested that Mr. Francis, who had been a 'tug' at
Eton, might care to examine us. Mr. Francis, who had
disapproved of my parents' system of home education,
saw his chance. He set us a Latin paper — translation,
grammar, composition. We floored it, as we thought,
with ease. But Mr. Francis was appalled. It appeared
that we had made do with one case, one tense, and one
declension throughout. It would not, he told my
father, be a question of taking Third Form; it would
be a question of failing altogether to get into Eton. My
father was greatly shaken and, rather unfairly, reproached
us for being both thick-headed and idle. Mr. Francis
asseverated that nothing but a tutor could save us. My
father agreed. But Mr. Francis' visit came to an end.
My mother intervened, and my father compromised by
writing to Ingalton-Drake's for the Eton Latin Grammar. For the next year that dark red volume, stamped
with the Eton arms, became our daily companion. So
unsophisticated were we, so uncorrupted by the 'small-
boy' values of a private school, that we looked upon
the Eton Latin Grammar as a sheet-anchor, a trusty
friend, a pilot that was to bring us into the haven where
we would be. For the name of Eton held magic for
us; Mr. Francis had scared us stiff; and from that time
onwards 'lessons' meant no longer so many hours of
duty, but so many hours of progression, led by the
Eton Latin Grammar, towards the Promised Land.
That we landed only in Middle Fourth was a blow to

my father's pride; but the credit for the fact that we landed at all must be divided between Mr. Francis Smith and Messrs. Ainger and Wintle.

My mother's veto on the tutor was not unwelcome to us. We could not picture Mr. Jenkins at the Chalet, where we had our meals, hugger-mugger, with the younger children and Lizzie Lee. Besides, we shared her confidence that her bright boys could not fail to pass into Eton. All little boys, she had explained to my father, learn Latin grammar; only her boys studied the ways of ants, patiently and intelligently, and were we not beginning to chat, easily and fluently, with Mr. Pitlou and with the menuisier, who taught us to dove-tail? Had we not visited those amazing pillars in the Val d'Hérens, each balancing a boulder upon its head, and seen the work of one of Arabella B. Buckley's Two Great Sculptors? Were we not enthusiastically pur-suing and observing the Swiss butterflies, the Apollos, the Commas, the Fritillaries, although denied, by her soft-heartedness, the coveted killing-bottle and the pin? Had we not found a salamander, that fabulous animal, all black and orange, the undoubted ancestor, if birds indeed had evolved from reptiles, of the golden oriole? And had we not, for all our youthful myopia, stood dumbfounded, when at a turn in the road above Evolena we had seen, glittering suddenly, a snowy pyramid, too perfect to be quite credible, which my father's map proved to be the Dent Blanche? Such experiences, in my mother's view, constituted education. Eton would take care of itself.

The close quarters of the Villa Dubochet, and the stark overcrowding in the Chalet, were transforming, by a subtle alchemy, our earlier conceptions of our parents. In Norfolk, although my mother had always governed, my father had reigned, nor had it ever entered our heads that he, too, might be one of the governed. His manifold cares of county and estate had separated him, for a greater part of the time, from our own workaday lives, and his prestige with the tenants and retainers, enhanced in our eyes by his great height and good looks, reinforced his standing with ourselves. If, on occasions, there was need to consult an oracle, he was the priest of Apollo. Except for a few stormy scenes in the schoolroom, he came among us relaxed and genial, omniscient but condescending, easily amused and often amusing. But here, in exile, landless, tenant-less, and without an occupation, he began to cut a different figure. An important function, in our new wandering way of life, was the management of transport. This was entirely in his hands. He had, fortunately, a passion for time-tables, especially continental ones; he studied them with zest, and could make them, miraculously, serve his purpose. Less fortunately, he was subject to attacks of train-fever of the most virulent kind. Arthur Christopher Benson once said of Dr. C. H. Lloyd, the music-master and precentor at Eton, that whereas the rest of us have to struggle with the beast within us, Lloyd contended with the bird within him. My father, when attacked by train-fever, had to struggle, like the rest of us Joneses, with the Celt within him. And the Celt, at his most excitable and unreasonable, always won. I have few more vivid memories of those restless years of travel than that of seeing my father, by a mountain of luggage, waving his arms at us, at the Chef de gare, at the porters, at the world in general, his features contorted and dissolving into a hundred criss-crossed lines, not of anger or excitement, but of mingled agony and sorrow. I came to think of it as his 'crucified look'. One could conceive of no grief, no physical torment, however excruciating, which could justify that aspect of ineluctable misery. Yet on no occasion was there the remotest of risks that we might miss a train. He had seen to that. Rather were we accustomed to spend long half-hours on the shallow platforms, where the sun blazed white and the station-bells tinkled monotonously, waiting, as far from the corrupting bookstalls as my mother could herd us, for the coming of the lordly foreign train.

At an amused word from my mother, the Celt lay down, and my father's countenance resumed its customary placidity. But I had been, momentarily, repelled and ashamed. A sense of humour, as distinguished from a sense of fun, is not often, I think, found in children. They condemn where an adult laughs, and become owlish and resentful over trifles. My father dancing on a platform is an amusing recollection, but for all that, he danced himself out of some part of my former absolute respect. I have no doubt that history has repeated itself, and that the Celt in me has often embarrassed my own children. Again, we soon discovered in the enforced intimacy of our unspacious 'lebensraum' that it was my mother, not my father, who had the last word on all occasions. He would propound some impulsive plan, and tell us that that, at any rate, was settled. We knew better. The two tall figures went off for a stroll together, 'a little turn,' they would call it, and in no time returned. My mother left it to my father to announce that the plan was 'off'; he had thought of some insuperable objections. But we knew perfectly whence those better, more practicable second thoughts had come.

The two years that passed between our going into exile and our going to Eton must, I think, have been for my mother years of signal happiness and self-fulfilment. She had us all bunched in her hand, as it were; there were no outside activities to distract her from the main object of all her thoughts and devotion: her family. We were more continuously under her eye than ever before; there were no long Cranmer passages, no broad staircase, to give notice of her approaching footfalls; she came suddenly among us at the turn of a door-handle; she could hear our moods through the slender walls; the lift towards her in unison of six smiling, loving faces, eager with prescribed affection, could be exacted and enjoyed at will. While carefully magnifying my father in our eyes, and gently closing him, as one closes a Bible, when we appeared to be reading with too much understanding the less edifying passages in his ever-open character, she used him, as I now know, to abet her in all her plans for us. They were two minds with but a single thought, but the thought was hers. We learnt from her authoritative lips how much we loved our parents and each other; how much we loved nature; how much we should, some day, love Matthew Arnold, and Ruskin, and Emerson, and George Macdonald, and the Arundel reproductions of the Italian painters. We might even hope, in a far future, to quote snatches of Goethe, like my father, or a few lines of Heine. Life could be all sweetness and light, if we would but take the mould she had in her mind for us. Meanwhile there must be absolute obedience to certain rules of behaviour; and as her eye was ever upon us, and we were as inept to seek the highest when we saw it as other children, there was a daily ration of checking, chiding, and correction. This was all in the day's work, and left no soreness; but the strain, as far as I myself was concerned, the unacknowledged oppression from which Eton proved to be so glorious a liberation, was the insistent exaction of signs and gestures and words of affection, the tokens of a surrender for which I had no mind. I could be happy without smiling, but smile I must; I could love without hugging, but hug I must. Nor, although I am confident that my mother was unaware of this, was there any room for diversity in her plan for the perfected family. She was always uneasy at any preference, any impulse, that ran counter to her own taste or values. A family, in her view, should have but one head and one heart. Outwardly, no mother could be less the dominant matriarch than was ours. Abnormally shy with strangers, gentle-mannered, tranquil and gay among her children, she was incapable of expressing, explicitly or implicitly, that it was her will that made our laws. If it was a case for authority, she saw to it that my father was invested with the 'imperium'; if it was a case for persuasion, she appealed to our consciences, confident that they would return the verdict she required; and indeed I cannot, in retrospect, for a moment suppose that my mother consciously moulded and fashioned us according to a model of her own choice. The pattern was laid up in Heaven; we must be taught to choose this and to like that because those things were right, not because she herself wished them. But as to what things were right, great or small, she was never for one moment in doubt. There is a hard core in most of us (possibly even in my elder sister, though I was never to discover it) which refuses to be conditioned, however insistent and insidious the hand that shapes us. And the perfect harmony for which my mother strove, and which she must have believed, in those years of our enforced propinquity beneath an alien sky, to have been achieved, was arrived at, in appearance, by means of our self-protecting hypocrisy alone; we continued to be, for all our vagrant tastes and fancies, the endearing 'yes-children' of our earlier days. Jesus could never have set us in the midst of His disciples, and bade them become like one of us. Rather would He have espied us peeping from behind the skirts of the Pharisees.

I have never ceased to wonder, in riper years, at the Christian Churches' insistence that the family is what they call 'the unit' of human society. No warrant for this opinion can be found in the words or acts of Jesus Himself. Indeed, on a famous occasion, He went out of His way to assert, in most emphatic terms, that the ties of kinship were as nothing beside the claims of like-mindedness. The family relationship is one we share with the animal world: immortal souls, in which the Churches so rightly, to my mind, believe, must surely have stronger affinities, a larger community, to search for, to be received into, and to enjoy. The parents of the body are unlikely, in the light of the available evidence, to be the parents of the soul; and a capacity for procreating by no means implies a capacity for educating. Nature does quite enough for the prestige of the family; a wise Church would, so far from abetting nature, be urgent in warning parents that each separate child is a 'unit' of society, solitary, lonely, and persistently in search of other birds of its own feather.

From this first year of our exile, then, when the great mountains hemmed us in, and the cramped interiors of Villa and Chalet compacted us physically, I must date the first cocking of a critical eye at my parents, hitherto sacrosanct. My father, always a lover of novelty, was in holiday mood, and expressed it by constant and sweeping assertions of how much better all things were ordered abroad. Why I was so fanatically and irrationally British I cannot tell; I am not sure that the basis of my patriotism was not squeamishness and the nausea I felt at foreign standards of sanitation, and at the outrageous use made of footpaths in the Canton of Valais. To this day I turn green if a puppy is sick in the hall, and in our prying and exploratory rambles my stomach was often turned. And there had been an abomination at a railway station. My father's enthusiasm for the manners of these foreigners, for their intelligence and vivacity, for the rich vocabulary of the peasants, for the lack of snobbery, for their good sense in sleeping after lunch and in sitting at little tables on the pavements, seemed to me superficial and thoughtless. What did all this amount to in a people who tolerated so much disgustfulness? There was a rule in our family that physical functions were presumed not to exist; in cases of absolute necessity my mother whispered, using euphemisms such as 'are you sure you are quite comfy?' before starting a journey, and it would have been unthinkable for me to comment upon my private feelings of revulsion. So that instead of openly declaring my grievances against these unclean people, and perhaps acquiring, by discussion, a sense of proportion, I accumulated resentment against my father's shallow views, and against his

apparent condonation of so much beastliness. I longed
to hear him praise our sweet, undefiled England. But
he never did. He went on extolling the foreigners'
art of living, and I durst not mention what so often
sickened me.

Against this resistance, always underground, and
largely provoked by our lack of elbow-room, must be
set the stimulus of my father and mother's conversation.
They travelled without a sense of history, but with an
eager eye for manners and differing ways of life, as well
as for natural beauty in every form, and for the common-
places of literary association. The Chalet was Mat
Arnold's plank-built cottage, backed by the pines, and
I was too young to know that 'plank-built' was perhaps
the ugliest sound in English poetry, not excepting
Milton's 'smooth-sliding Mincius'. My father had a
smattering of geology, and discoursed about strata, and
glaciers, and Lyell, and Tyndall; he had more than a
smattering of field botany. All these were lunch-time
topics, after a morning spent with my mother learning
German by the Gouin system of suiting the action to
the word. 'Ich hebe mein rechtes Bein auf. Ich setze
mein rechtes Bein an. Ich nehme so einen Schritt,' we
had repeated, high-stepping in slow time round the
tiny sitting-room. But the liberality of my parents'
thought was more strikingly reflected in their habit of
discussing, in our presence, the fundamental problems
of religion. Like all sensible people who really care
about these grave matters, they were constantly re-
shaping their conception of God, and they wished us,
young as we were, to share their preoccupations. My
father, for all his enjoyment of reading the Lessons,
which he did most impressively, had become more and

more restive under the yoke of obligatory church-going in Norfolk. Once he had tumbled to the colossal misunderstanding begotten by the translation of the name 'Yahveh' as 'the Lord', with all its deplorable consequences in identifying a cruel and warlike tribal deity with the Heavenly Father of the New Testament, he had boldly neglected the lectionary and treated the docile congregation to the poetry of Isaiah or the Book of Job. But, always a lover of phrases, he had somewhere come across the description of churches as 'liturgical traps', and he refused, ever after, to be caught in them. 'Blue domer' was another fashionable transatlantic phrase at that time which appealed to him. He still read to us on Sunday mornings from the Gospels, with a particular love of the Fourth Gospel, but the words 'Higher Criticism' were becoming familiar to us, and we were gradually absorbing, from our parents' talk, the point of view that the Bible, Old and New Testaments alike, was not the Word of God but the words of men, fallible and groping, about God. For this early emancipation of our consciences from subjection to a Book and its inflexible Author I am truly grateful, as for the conviction that religion, in the broadest sense of the word, is much too momentous a subject to be left to clergymen. It is the dearest concern of each of us, and must be grappled with, not vicariously, but by every man for himself.

So now, eighteen hundred and ninety-six years after the birth of Jesus, this tight little, right little English family was living in the keeping, and the eye, of a God still Protestant, but no longer clerical-minded or particular about forms of worship. When we attended, as occasion offered, morning service in one of those prim

little Anglican churches where the chaplain beamed at
us for doubling his congregation at a blow, we repeated
the Apostles' Creed with simple faith in all the clauses
save those which confess a belief in the Holy Catholic
Church and in the Resurrection of the Body. These
my parents were unable to swallow, so we, too, could
not swallow them; and we quietly omitted them, not
without, in my own case, a grain of self-satisfaction at
knowing better than the dear old ladies on either hand.
But we were sure of this: that God watched us and
marked what we did amiss, and that His intentions for
us and the world could be changed by prayer. I did
not love Him, because the test of love, for me, was a
wish for the loved one's constant companionship, and
there could be no question but that the constant companionship of God would have been a greater strain
upon me than I could have borne. But I acknowledged
His omnipotence and omniscience, and was already
suspecting that those parts of Scripture that attributed
to Him actions and thoughts that fell short even of
human goodness could not be true. And I think I
already began to associate the idea of Him with the
beauty of the visible world; not with the starry heavens,
not with the mountains that can move grown men, but
with the crocus-cup and the peacock butterfly. Young
eyes are focused on what can be touched at arm's
length; one has to grow up to grandeur. And of
Nature red in tooth and claw, of her sublime and fright-
ening indifference to the individual man or mouse, I
was still unaware.

While our parents' table-talk was enlarging our
minds in some directions, in others this period was, for
us boys, one of backsliding. Deliberately protected,
I

as we had been, from the debasing impact of massed small boys at a private school, we were none the less falling away from our pristine levels of taste and imagination in books. Was it from the workings of that inner schoolboy which seems to lurk in the 'unconscious' of even the home-bred? Or was it simply that while books for children had been, in the last years of the century, written by authors with singular gifts of story-telling, of style, of historical imagination, the writers for boys happened, by pure chance, to be less well endowed? However that may be, it is undeniable that to forsake Charles Kingsley's *Water Babies* and *Heroes*, Charlotte Yonge's *Lances of Lynwood*, Louisa Alcott's *Little Men*, Mrs. Ewing's *Jackanapes*, Hawthorne's *Tanglewood Tales*, and Lewis Carroll's *Alice* for G. A. Henty and Ballantyne, was to exchange silver, if not gold, for copper. We made the descent unawares. *With Clive in India*, *With Wolfe in Canada* seemed to us capital tales, and no doubt they were. Kingston's *The Three Midshipmen* was better still. We had temporarily lost touch, in the labyrinth of heartiness, with the saving thread of art. Fortunately, R. L. S. was there, down among the hearties, to pick up the thread for us.

We were also, it must be confessed, not quite up to the level of our opportunities. Had we been five years younger or five years older, I think our imaginations and sympathies could have been enlarged by these years of exile. But we, who had been romantics, were now rat-killers and would-be sportsmen. There was nothing for us to hunt among the larches of Les Mayens. At Clarens we had, it is true, caught perch from the pier to which ropes were thrown from the *William Tell* or the *Winkelried* as the paddle-wheels backed and

churned. It had been sport of a kind; but when September came round, we sighed for the smell of cordite,
wafted over the roots in the sharp morning air.

Moreover, I am sorry to say, we were already
infected by that most blighting of boy-sicknesses, the
desire to be 'ordinary'. This miserable ambition, which
attacks English boys like the measles, was beginning to
diminish our mental and emotional stature, and to come
between us and our blessings. We felt anything but
'ordinary', with our shock heads, our relentless long
walks on the slippery, pine-needled slopes, a maid who
wore no cap or apron, and an unoccupied father who
everlastingly praised the eccentric and unfastidious ways
of these foreign people. Incurious and prosaic, our
small minds pined for a punt upon the River Wensum,
while our high-minded and unconventional parents
were congratulating themselves upon our exposure to
the richness and variety of our new way of life.

I doubt if the exultation with which a Winthrop
Young used to return to the precipices of the Grépon
or the Grandes Jorasses could exceed that felt by ourselves when we descended to the floor of the Rhône
Valley, and to the flat meadows, empurpled with
autumn crocus, at Bex-les-Bains. At this dull little
place, made pleasant by walnut-trees, we spent a few
weeks in the rapture of a convalescence free, at long last,
from pain. With the cool autumn days the thunder-
storms that had hunted and haunted us at Les Mayens
came no more; and there were crayfish in the irrigation
ditches which we caught by the dozen by dangling over
them butchers' lights held in a cleft stick. It was not
so exciting as ratting, but the crayfish, being edible,
were legitimate prey, and my mother need have no

misgivings about our blood-thirstiness. And it was at
Bex that we first learnt not to judge our fellow-creatures
by their appearance. There was a French boy of fourteen staying by himself at the Pension. His hair was
plastered back; he wore gold pince-nez; he had an
unbelievable poise. Our first evening, when he took
his seat at his separate table, looked coolly at the new
arrivals and unfolded his napkin with a great play of
long pale hands and an air, insufferable to us, of weary
insouciance, we wrote him down as a poseur and a
prig. But next morning he joined us, of his own
accord, in the garden. He was entirely delightful, gay,
natural, friendly, and adventurous. He offered to show
us the salt mines. We borrowed candlesticks and
walked behind Georges, in single file, half a mile or
more into the heart of the mountain. He became our
leader and our hero. We had learnt that deportment
and a studied manner, even pince-nez, can go with a
merry and an enterprising heart.

While we were rejoicing in this life on the level,
and being treated for massed mosquito-bites, which
made us look like portraits by Seurat and turned out to
be chickenpox, our parents were planning a winter of
intensive culture for us at Baden-Baden. Baden-Baden
did not make a good carrot for my mother to dangle
before us. We had been 'had' over the Mayens de
Sion; we were becoming increasingly British, sighing
for marmalade and bacon for breakfast. Something
was said about skating, but we had only hobbled on
the inside edge on the Cranmer ponds, and we knew
that the skating was a blind. If we went to Baden-
Baden, a forbidding sort of name anyhow, it would
be to learn German, and here we were already deeply

involved with French and Latin, and in the early stages of Greek. So it was with enormous relief that we learnt that my mother had dreamt one night that a great porcelain stove was crushing her to death. Until that nightmare was sent to her by our guardian angels she had forgotten, in her concern for our minds, that Baden-Baden would be heated, not by fragrant wood fires, but by stoves. And it seems she remembered a fire of pine-cones that had crackled gaily at Le Maquis, a villa at Valescure, and had sufficed to make habitable, for all its feebleness, rooms already warmed by the Riviera's winter sunshine. Valescure was another sort of carrot altogether; there would be sea-bathing at St-Raphael, and boating and sea-fishing; there would be green lizards and water-tortoises; there would be no German; it had a lovely name, and it lay among the foothills of the Esterels, a lovelier name still.

So the dancing and waving upon platforms began again, and ended in the Grand Hôtel at Valescure, and I still remember our arrival before dusk, and the exhilaration of our first plunge into the *maquis*. Cistus and myrtle and butcher's berry clothed the miniature ravines; the little pines were green and feathery, as unlike as could be from the stiff and regimented young silver that had been planted to succeed our Rookery elms; the nest of the processional caterpillar hung here and there among their branches; and the smooth, rounded rocks in the half-dry watercourses slid into sunlit pools where little tortoises swam. The great mountains had failed to conquer us, but to this sweet-smelling, child-size country we instantly surrendered. There were no fences, hedges, or monitory notice-boards; there was nothing to hinder our exploration of these mild but deeply wrinkled foothills between the plain of Fréjus and the distant mountain of Ste-Baume; and the great umbrella pines stood up on ridge and promontory to guide and orientate us in our serpentine wanderings. Sudden conversions are, after all, not so rare; and this was a clear case of the sort. We, who at Les Mayens had been sighing for a weedy Norfolk river and the shallow bathing pool at the bend where the alders grow, abandoned, at the first sight and smell of the cistus and the pine, the myrtle and the cork-oak, our disgruntlement and our hankerings, and were even, more strangely still, content to let our hunting instincts have a rest. The common lizards, studded with tur-quoises along their sucking flanks, the Scarcer Swallow-tail butterfly, the Trap-door spider, the Oleander hawk-moth, the green tree-frog, all these delightful creatures satisfied our cravings for pursuit, and reproached, with their beauty, any lurking wish to kill. And at night, when the frogs were loud and incessant in the plain of Fréjus, we heard, from the warm pine-woods that undulated upwards to Mont Vinaigre, the single, unvarying hoot of the little Scops owl.

We did not know then that my father a couple of years later was to build his own villa at Valescure; but had we known it, we should have been perfectly con-tent. As the blue sky to Coleridge's stars, so did this Ligurian landscape seem, in our first enthusiasm, to be our appointed rest and our native country and our own natural home. For small boys from Norfolk already slightly soiled with xenophobia and but a week ago inclined to think that 'abroad' was much overrated, it was a notable conversion.

The spell of the countryside was assisted, no doubt,

by other considerations. Living conditions were transformed. My father hired a villa with the not uncommon name of 'Mon Repos', but, unlike the Villa
Dubochet, it was high and square and spacious, with
marble steps and marble pavements, and we no longer
had to live on top of one another. Its enormous garden
was mostly a thicket of great heaths and cistus, shadowed
by Mediterranean pines, but there were tall eucalyptus
and umbrella pines to give us dignity, and oleanders in
tubs upon the balustraded terrace. It looked west over
the Maures mountains and the cloven hump of Roque-
brune, and south over St-Raphael and the sea. We
had our own schoolroom. We had our English cook,
Sarah. And best of all, we helped to found and manage
the Royal Valescure Yacht Club. (Burgee: dark blue
cross on white.) For Valescure, in those days, consisted of two hotels, less than a score of English villas,
and a 'Site for the English Chur'. (Although the
notice-board was never, the English Church has since
been, completed.) And, owing to its smallness, it was
a neighbourly and sociable settlement. Mr. Henry
Bullock Hall, of Six-Mile-Bottom, was a permanent
winter migrant in Le Maquis, with his French wife
and lovely daughters Lisa and Sybille. His head buzzed
with Roman remains about which he wrote and discoursed interminably, with Forum Julii as his home-
quarry, while Mrs. Hall lamented: 'the worst of taking
Henery to church, it is so long before he will go again'.
But Lisa, lovely Lisa, tall and slender, with the face of
an archangel, taught us to draw and paint boats in the
sunny anglicised sitting-room of Le Maquis, teaching
us that, as regards the men in the boat, you must attend
to their square shoulders and the heads will take care of

themselves. (I can still draw a fisherman in a boat with moderate competence.) On the hillock above Le Maquis dwelt M. le Pasteur Goulden, of Sedan, endowed with the profits of champagne, with his sisters Mlle Augustine and Mlle Lucie. Mlle Augustine was formidable, with hair tightly drawn back into a bun, and irritated her brother by reminding him out of turn, when the dish was particularly to his taste, to remember his 'mal d'estomac'. 'Mais tais-toi, Augustine, je n'ai pas de mal d'estomac, moi', he would pipe up in his high tenor, so ill-matched with his great bulk. But Mlle Lucie, whose face was like yours or mine reflected in the back of a table-spoon, was all friendliness and charm, and brought out sweet biscuits from tall dressers of polished walnut. M. le Pasteur, whose tiny eyes beamed joyfully in a round face crinkled with bonhomie, used sometimes to hold a short Protestant service on Sunday mornings in his dining-room, to which we were taken. I was already old enough to notice how much the Gospel stories suffered, in the French language, from the lack of the majestic cadences of our own Authorised Version. But his piety was cheerful and unparsonic, and suited my parents: and the light refreshments that followed the brief sermon suited us.

But these were elderly people even to our parents. For ourselves, the thing that made permanent our love at first sight for this fair ground onto which our lot had fallen, was the companionship of other children. Except for one memorable week at Dunston with the beautiful Buxtons, when I had fallen in love with Joan but been affianced to Olive (who was of a more suitable age, since seven hesitates to propose to twelve), and for that fortnight at Bex-les-Bains in the suite of the elegant Georges, we had seen next to nothing of children of our own age. And when, after due enquiries and inspection, we were allowed to go for walks by ourselves with Geoffrey Sturt and his two sisters, already in their teens, our suppressed sociability burst out like a torrent in spate. We did not, at first, want to play games; we wanted to talk and to compare notes; we wanted to talk, above all, about books. We wanted to speculate about marriage. Geoffrey, who had been long at a private school, had, his sisters assured us, a theory. Geoffrey, pressed for his theory, temporised. He was not sure; he would rather hear our views. But we had none. The girl Sturts believed that it had something to do with sharing a bed, and we were greatly interested. There was a dreadful moment when this delightful friendship all but crashed. We were discussing R. L. S., and the Sturts described for us the story of *The Body-Snatchers*. We boys were thrilled. But my elder sister was greatly perturbed. She did not think it was the kind of story of which my mother would approve. It lacked sweetness and light. That night, when my mother went to her bedroom to say good-night, my sister's swelling conscience could carry her secret no longer. She wept, and blew the gaff. My mother was appalled. She consulted my father, who confirmed that R. L. S. had indeed written the story. 'But,' said my mother to us all, 'he would never have breathed it, even to me.' The Sturts must have horrid minds. They were all but warned off. But our despair moved her. She took into consideration that R. L. S. had written *Virginibus Puerisque* and a score of wholesome, breezy, manly books. The Sturts were within their

rights to read and to love him. They may have
stumbled upon this evil story unwittingly. But the
ugly fact remained that they had retailed it to innocent
young friends. Perhaps my father put in a word; at
any rate my mother relented, and we were allowed to
continue the acquaintance, but with strict orders to
refuse, in future, to listen to anything horrid. To such
a degree were we guarded. But the Royal Valescure
Yacht Club, for all that Geoffrey Sturt was a staunch
supporter and co-editor of the *Valescure Yachtsman*, the
Club's organ, had its genesis with another family.

Close by the Villa Clythia, beneath a red cliff, was
Valescure's only pond. Here we sailed toy boats,
bought at St-Raphael; here we built a harbour and a
lighthouse. Out from the Villa Clythia ran Billy and
Tommy and Jacky Cecil, trailing aunts. These aunts
who, like ourselves, came from Norfolk, were more
spirited, more boyish, more inventive, more fond of
play, even than their nephews. They were aunts who
went annually to Cowes. They knew about burgees
and spinnakers and Commodores. We must, said the
aunts, have a Club. They cut out and sewed spinnakers
for us all. They substituted for our lighthouse built of
mud a tall, tapering white lighthouse made of wood,
with small black windows. They drew up rules. They
gave prizes for races, and entertained the Club at tea.
They bought and read and contributed to the *Valescure
Yachtsman*. They talked broad Norfolk, or cockney,
and made us laugh. They enlivened our existence.
'Doubtless God could have made better aunts, but
doubtless He never did.'

We were within a year, now, of going to Eton. We
should, by all the rules of the nineties, have been play-

ing Association football under the eyes of a games-
master, not sailing toy boats on a pond in the company
of spinster ladies. But I am sure that, as a preparation
for Eton, we had the better part. Sib and Flo and Maggie
Amherst, childlike, witty, ingenious, travelled, lovers of
sport and games and beauty and people, were, to my
mind, the perfect companions for a boy of twelve.
They valued the great world, in which they lived in
wealth and splendour, for what it was worth; and
brought to the business of living an eager gaiety, a
quick eye for the pith and point of things, which could
not fail to attract and infect a boy. Through them I
got an inkling, however unconsciously, of the art of
sifting, in a complex world, the gold from the dross.

Meanwhile our parents were doing their best, as we
saw it, to go native. They dined with, and asked to
dinner, a young French architect and his wife. (They
were yet to learn that, in those days in France, 'archi-
tecte!' was a worse term of abuse than 'assassin' to hurl
at an enemy.) They were full of the verve and intelligence of the professional classes in France, so different
from the dull conventionality of their British counter-
parts. They enjoyed talking French, my mother cor-
rectly, my father fluently but regardless of genders. But
so strong was the spell of Valescure that now, while
still resenting the slights upon my dear England, of
which I knew about two square miles, I no longer
reacted, as in Switzerland, against the natives. Valescure was clean; and the early impression of France
made by Georges Deloche and *Les Mots historiques* was
confirmed by the Provençal sunshine that pierced our
green shutters and by the warmth of the garde cham-
pêtre, Monsieur Suche. We had been shocked, on our

first meeting, at finding finches in his game-bag, and still more shocked to see a string of gold-crested wrens hanging in the market at St-Raphael, but his cheerful greeting of 'Ohé la jeunesse!' and his friendly interest in our green frogs and chrysalises, won us over to this calm and solid Frenchman who, as far as his outward appearance went, might well have been a Norfolk gamekeeper. And when a telegram arrived one night as we sat at dessert, and my father said 'Rather anxious news' and took my mother into the drawing-room, whence we heard, through the thin French double-doors, the rise and fall of their voices in prolonged, disturbing colloquy, we learnt, without emotion, that Mr. Fisher was dead, and that my parents must return to England at once. Had we known that Mr. Fisher had hanged himself at the Home Farm, it might have been different, but we had not forgiven that stout, black-avised bailiff for barking at Stanley to remember that we were little gentlemen, and his death brought us one of those refreshing interludes of liberty and relaxation. It was pleasant to dangle one's legs from the kitchen-table and gossip with Sarah and the moon-faced Auguste, and to be low-brows among lower-brows, and to have the Sturts to tea unmindful of the censorship. We felt like clergymen on holiday, without their round collars.

At Christmas my elder brother and I fell in love. It was with Lisa who, in Greek draperies, stood upon a plinth as Galatea during charades. We had in turn been pressed to play Pygmalion and to woo her, and had refused, with burning cheeks. My younger brother took the part, and had won much applause for his portrayal of passion when, by lying on his back and kicking his legs in the air, he finally brought life into her marble loveliness, and induced her to step, with infinite slow grace, from the draped music-stool into his short, hot arms. His performance revolted us. I had never seen such beauty as was Lisa's that night: 'vera incessu patuit dea'. Gilda's chest was forgotten. My brother and I undressed in silence. From his bed, in the dark, came the betraying question: 'If you had to marry Maud or Lisa, which would you marry?' 'Maud!' I lied. 'So would I', he lied back. Maud was a charming grown-up cousin at the Villa-les-Pins, and I knew why she had been dragged in. Only by such a ruse could he have brought up the new-loved name with which our young hearts were preoccupied. Only so could he have coupled that name with marriage. And, of course, only in the dark. But I felt relief that the conjunction had been effected, without compromising my private vision of felicity, and I cannot think that he, in his bed, was deceived. Maud, my foot!

Lisa was half-French, and France scored still further points when the warm weather came and the springs of our happiness shifted from the foothills to the bathing-establishment of the brothers Lambert at St-Raphael. The false Frenchmen we had been so hot upon at Agincourt had been small of stature, five of them to one Englishman in the scales. But the brothers Lambert were, physically, the finest men we had ever seen. One dark, the other fair, they were tall and broad and more muscular than Mr. Jenkins. Their deep bass voices, their great chests beneath white cotton singlets, were stupendously manly. They had the grand manner. They were calm yet alert and, undeniably, Frenchmen. Under their friendly eyes, in the warm buoyant Mediterranean, we became strong and confident swimmers.

They were transformed, as the years went by, from heroes into cronies. I shall never forget them; I had thought they could never have forgotten us. Twenty-two years later, a few months after the armistice, I had occasion to revisit St-Raphael. I hurried to the Bains de Mer. The brothers Lambert were still there. Shrunken, starved, with anxious, indifferent eyes, the thin dark brother and the haggard fair one came forward to be at my service. I gripped their hands. I told them my name. No flicker of recognition came. After explanations, they admitted some faint recollections. But they were not interested. They had served in the French navy, but now there was no proper 'nourriture'. In these scarecrow strangers I recognised at last what the first Great War had done to the French people.

There was a dead kingfisher in the boat when we rowed up the Argens from Fréjus, and when we exclaimed over its brilliance, the boatman shook his head and said 'pas bon à manger'. France lost a few points there; but out at sea, when we pulled up fish as dazzling as any kingfisher, we acknowledged no falling away from British standards because these spiny, rainbow creatures were also not worth the cooking. We English know that all fishing, but only some shooting, is sport; the French have yet to achieve this mark of civilisation. They even have the bad taste to eat that horrible small octopus, the 'squid'. We enjoyed tempting him out of his hole in the red volcanic rocks with a bait tied to the end of a long bamboo pole. It was good fun to peer down into the limpid, translucent pools, and to watch those odious tentacles grope for, and embrace, the pale, waving rag of fish-gut. But to declare the creature 'bon à manger' instead of catching him for sport alone — that, we felt, was a bit much. But for the sake of Lisa, of the brothers Lambert, of Valescure, of Georges, of the *Mots historiques*, I, for one, was not going to be unduly upset by these imperfections.

One more physical experience of those days must be set down, if only to prove that this was 1897. It was Cousin Charlie Allix who first tasted the new thrill, and could not rest till we had shared it. Tall and gaunt, with hair inexplicably but undeniably green, Charlie Allix owned a high-frame bicycle which, when the red tracks petered out, he carried upon his great back for miles across the ravines of the Esterel. He was the father of that Maud whom my brother and I had so shamelessly used as camouflage for our true heart's desire, but Captain Young, who had rebuked us for 'putting on side' (a strange new expression) when he met us riding on the boulevard with our hands off the handlebars, had wooed and won Maud, and I do not think she was in the procession that toiled behind Cousin Charlie, each man or boy or girl pushing a bicycle, all the weary uphill miles to the very shoulder of Mont Vinaigre. Here there was a little wayside cabaret, and we lunched off dried figs from a great stone jar, and that most delicious of all breads, the grey, crusty, double 'flute'. And because water in France might not be safe, even we children had a glass of red wine. The taste of that meal, eaten among the pines, under a Mediterranean sky, has lasted a lifetime. Then came the great moment. We turned our bicycles off the narrow, gritty road of our ascent, onto the smooth breadth of the Route Nationale. 'Like a billiard-table,' said Cousin Charlie. A few turns of the pedals, then up went our feet onto the 'rests' (there were no free-wheels in those days) and we coasted down, five or six miles, leaning right or left to the bold curves of the road, tasting the wind, ecstatic and vainglorious. Did we do fifteen miles to the hour? I have no idea. But it was our first acquaintance with speed, and we felt like swallows. A year or two later we stood at the side of this same Route Nationale, to see the horseless carriages go by in the first race from Marseilles to Nice. The devilish, delightful things were doing up to thirty miles an hour, the pace at which Dr. Johnson said the human frame must collapse.

That summer my father, prancing and gesticulating, transported us to Aargau in northern Switzerland. Here, on its own wooded pyramid, stood Schloss Wildegg, above the yellow Aar River. This ancient stronghold of some robber baron, poised for mischief, had a Rittersaal where suits of armour stood in rows like men. We should have been glad had it been possible to avoid the Rittersaal after dusk, but it was not possible. We had to whistle, instead, as we passed through it to the gloomy, spiral stairs. Had we come to inhabit Schloss Wildegg in the days of our romantic childhood, when *Anne of Geierstein* was our reading, and the clash of men-at-arms our play, I think we should have appreciated more fully our privilege in dwelling in a castle little changed, save in furnishings, since the Middle Ages. But Eton was approaching; Mr. Meneer had been engaged, fresh from some scholastic triumph for which his photograph had appeared in the cutting sent by Gabbitas and Thring, to ensure that we should take Remove; we wanted to fish, and above all to bathe, in the trout-streams on the plain

below us; and I think we were more resentful of the
daily toil up the steep path and steps to our feudal
fortress than charmed by the grandeur and panache
of our summer home. And I, for my part, had a vague,
uneasy feeling that we did not belong there. It was not
our coat-of-arms that was carved upon its stones, again
and again, wheresoever a coat-of-arms could, by in-
genuity, be put. My hand never went to my hip as I
stood before that heraldic doorway and looked across
to the Hapsburg keep that crowned a neighbouring
rock. I should like to have been the thirty-fourth
Graf Effinger of Wildegg, not a sub-tenant of Colonel
Rivett-Carnac. Too old any longer to project myself,
imaginatively, into the role of a feudal lord, I was still
unripe for the recognition that there had been more
illustrious warriors, with bluer blood, than this twelve-
year-old younger son of a Norfolk squire.

The Baroness Effinger herself, the last of her race,
lived in a small house just below the Castle. She
looked every inch not a Baroness. Square, Germanic,
dowdy, she complained that our bicycles, left leaning
against the wall of her cowhouse, made the butter taste
of oil. We did not take to her at all. Mr. Meneer, on
the other hand, whose drooping moustache in the
photograph had faintly disconcerted us, was a great
success. My parents afterwards complained that he
was impervious to beauty; they had given him a free
trip to Interlaken, and he had not, it seemed, noticed
the Jungfrau. But he delighted in swimming, as we
did; and we learnt from him, as we bathed together,
stark naked in a sheltered pool, the insignia of manhood.
This interested us much. Mr. Meneer was definitely
hirsute. And his tranquil, confident teaching of Latin

K

and Greek and Algebra confirmed us in our feeling that we should take Remove, in spite of his kindly warnings that perhaps it would only be Fourth Form. He was patient and equable, and, like us, amused at foreigners and the way they made themselves at home in these distant parts. For this was German Switzerland, and for the first time since we had come abroad we were among natives with whom we could not talk, not even with the cook, not even by raising our voices.

Herr Kim, the village schoolmaster, came three mornings a week in order to remedy this state of affairs. He got very hot climbing the hill; his hair was cut 'en brosse', and he wore gold-rimmed spectacles. He was infinitely kindly and patient, but his simple little tales of a Knabe who was krank, and recovered on being given a Kaninchen, did not provide us with the vocabulary required for getting our bicycles mended. We thought him a little childish. He did, however, invite us to join his school in an outing. This turned out to be a feat of endurance almost beyond our powers. It began badly, because in the train that took us, all one long hot day, south through the St-Gothard tunnel, we were the victims of our blonde, shaven-headed companions in a trick that revolted our very souls. A bunch of them, in a carriage forward of our own, leaned out together, amassing spittle. A confederate in our carriage, at a given moment, urged us to put our heads out of the window in order to admire some crag or some cascade, and the hoarded spittle, suddenly released into the wind-slip, slapped into our eyes. The spit-shooters were Swiss, but they spoke German, and I have an idea that I did not feel altogether clean from that outrageous defilement until November 11, 1918. It was small comfort when one of the cropped savages lost his straw hat and cried for half the morning.

At Airolo, at the southern end of the St-Gothard tunnel, we lay on mattresses in a kind of attic, but were kept from sleep by fleas. At 3 a.m. we began, with lanterns, our long trudge over the St-Gothard pass. We breakfasted in the Hospice, with bearded monks to pour the coffee, and drifts of dirty snow beside the road. We were deathly tired all day. At some point on the downward road we climbed into a diligence, and had the thrill of descending, at a gallop, round precipitous curves and across the Devil's Bridge. But when, in the blazing afternoon, we embarked in a steamer on the Lake of lovely Lucerne, we slept, achingly, on the narrow benches, sickened by scenery. There was no singing when the exhausted band arrived, crumpled and red-eyed, at Wildegg. Can it have been such a 'treat' as this that wrung from a little boy that *cri-de-cœur*: 'Our Lord said: "Suffer little children", and oh how they do suffer?'

That summer was sultry, and I had some difficulty in persuading myself, in my bed in a vast unshuttered library, that I was too old to be afraid of thunder-storms, for the continuous lightning made sinister the gaunt and tortured shapes of the massive furniture. As a bedroom, the library was anything but snug, and thunder is best countered by cosiness. And I knew that, downstairs in the Rittersaal, the suits of armour were watching and waiting. I did not relish those hot nights at Wildegg.

For all that, I had developed, since the days of the Chalet, new powers of appreciation. I found the storks, perched on the neat church-towers, enchanting, and I was genuinely thrilled when, bicycling upon the plain, we crossed a river by a covered wooden bridge that had remained untouched since the fourteenth century. And I fell, at last, under the spell of high mountains. From our Schloss we could see, on clear evenings after rain, away to the south, the rosy snow summits of the Oberland giants. My mother had taught us the Lorelei song, and these peaks seemed to me to be the very gipfels that had funkeled in the abend sonnenschein of that pensive and melancholy ditty. I used to gaze at them, if possible in solitude, and to feel immortal longings. They made me ache with their beauty, as they shone, majestic and withdrawn, on the uttermost rim of my visible world. Those far-off mountains could quieten at times, as the summer evenings died, the whole family; but they belonged, I thought, to me.

It was at Wildegg that we children came, for the first time in our lives, within feeling distance of death. It was not a personal sorrow, but it was disturbing, because it struck at the seemingly invulnerable. 'Gus' Jessup, a friend of my parents and a neighbour both at Valescure and at Schloss Lenzburg, that nobler edition of Wildegg upon a near-by hill, was suddenly bereaved. A telegram came from Valescure that Lady Mildred was dead. We had seen Mr. Jessup quite lately at Lenzburg. He was an American, enormous, yellow-haired, rubicund, blue-eyed, jolly. My mother, who was much shaken by compassion for this big, helpless man, talked to us freely. We knew that he had, when my parents visited him, laid his head upon the table and sobbed. The picture haunted me. I saw that great yellow head bowed in misery. His size, for some obscure reason, made it worse in my eyes. Was it that

there was so much of him to suffer? I had scarcely
seen Lady Mildred, who was an invalid, but I was never
quite so young again after she died. Twelve months
later, I was to learn that there can be grief too great for
tears.

Our departure from Wildegg was hurried. There
had been some days of horror when a pair of ducks in
the kitchen had become 'high' and, although promptly
buried in the woods, had left their ghosts to haunt every
room in the Castle. But now a new smell began to
creep from room to room. The Baroness Effinger
alone could detect nothing wrong. She came and
sniffed, but it was the sniff of scepticism. But my
father firmly said 'Sewer gas', and we fled to our dear
Pension Crochet at Bex. But the spell was broken.
There was no Georges to lead us; we were no longer
avid to feel the earth level beneath our feet, and we
were impatient for Valescure. Only one memory survives. A group of pleasant, grown-up French people,
with whom my parents had made friends at the Pension,
offered one evening to act a Charade. 'What fun,'
said my mother, 'and how good for the children to
see and hear!'—for she had been assured that nothing
unsuitable for the 'jeune fille' should be touched upon.
And they were as good as their word. And yet — the
word to be acted was 'Cabriolet', the last syllable was
'lait'. A wet-nurse was to be engaged. The part was
taken by a delightful young Frenchman. His bosom
was swelling and realistic. But the prospective employer was cautious. 'Vous avez beaucoup de lait?'

'Mais si, j'en ai beaucoup.'

'Alors, montrez-moi votre lait' — and the wet-
Frenchman's bodice was clawed open, to unload an

avalanche of cushions. We children roared; but my mother's face was red. She knew that we had seen nourrices in action beneath the plane-trees that shaded the lake-side at Clarens, but she felt, I am sure, that the French, so apt to become too French, had done it once again.

We journeyed south in stages. We stopped at Geneva, at Lyons, at Vienne. Why do I remember the 'Maison Carrée', that exquisite Roman temple, to this day? Was this the first occasion on which the sudden sight of a building, if it had proportion and symmetry and grace, gave me, as so many hundreds of times since, a sharp, instantaneous sensation of high delight? Was it at Vienne that the germ was sown that was to infect me, many years later, with shame for my grandfather? with shame for Cranmer itself, whose Georgian simplicity that grandfather, swayed by fashion, had paid Philip Webb to mutilate? We had been taken to see Cathedrals, and we recognised that the Castle of Chillon looked well against the blue lake and the Dent du Midi; but, until we came to Vienne, I have no remembrance of responding spontaneously, and unbidden, to the magic of a building.

At Vienne we embarked, the only passengers, upon a Rhône cargo-boat, and sat delightedly upon bales and packing-cases as we steamed, in that narrow black vessel, as far as Avignon. At Lyons we had seen the Rhône and the Saône, after their still unconsummated marriage, flowing side by side in one channel, like bride and bridegroom coming down the aisle, the Rhône, as bride, ice-blue and clear, the bridegroom Saône brown and muddied. But now the two were one, swift and strong, and my father must have felt rewarded by our pleasure and excitement for his admirable decision to take to the river.

At Avignon, unluckily, although we managed to dance upon the broken bridge to the tune of the old song, the mistral blew in full force. The cypresses were bending, the dust swirled; the sun blazed, as always on days of mistral, upon the bleached hills and the brown Palace of the Popes, and we were tossed and battered about beyond endurance. The mistral is a damnable wind, for all that it brings fine weather; even at Valescure, where it has turned the corner and rushes at you from the west, it rattles and bangs the shutters for three days and nights on end, and is altogether merciless. Prayer does no good; through such a hubbub, it would seem, God cannot hear a word you say. There is nothing to be done about the mistral but to wait till it blows itself out.

At Toulon we rowed out to a French warship, the *Brennus*, and were shown over the ship. Some of the officers and men wore moustaches, and we knew how a second Trafalgar would go. How did my father work these things? He was never a shy man, but to board, with a family of six, a foreign man-of-war, and to be received with warmth, seems to me a notable piece of enterprise.

And so back to our dear Valescure, where 'Gus' Jessup, to make Remove more sure, coached us in Algebra. I was embarrassed at sitting with this bulky sorrowful man, clothed all in black, but perhaps he found relief in the impersonal austerities of simple equations. He it was, moreover, who helped to persuade my father to buy a few acres of pine-wood and cistus, on which to build his own villa. We knew, at

last, that we were not going back to Norfolk. The
'overdraft' had already swum into our ken, at first as a
distant cloud, no bigger than a man's hand, but to loom
menacingly, in years to come, over our tender consciences. My father confessed to being 'poor', so we
were poor too; not beggars, of course, but slightly
'déclassés', owning no horses, no men-retainers except
a boy in a blouse. At the Villa Clythia, 'Oh, Edwin'
and Richard wore livery and crested buttons to carry
in the tea-table; but our liveries were being devoured
by moths in a Cranmer attic, and our front-door was
answered (strange phrase) by a maid who wore no cap.
Visitors did not seem to mind, but this was their politeness, no doubt. What was more curious, my parents
did not seem to care a button. They appeared to think
that life was pleasanter when there were no men-
servants to appease, for the apologetic address of 'Oh,
Edwin', which gave his name to the Clythia footman —
what was it but appeasement? But I was, privately,
not quite so sure. Might not this contentment with
capless French maids be only one more symptom of
those anti-British tendencies for which my father was
suspect? In England people like us had butlers. And
even in rectories and at Camberley, where my grandmother lived, the parlourmaids wore caps. I had not
heard, then, about explorers who dressed for dinner
every evening in the African jungle, but, unconsciously,
I belonged to their school of thought, except that in
my case it was not self-respect but Nationalism that I
was for safeguarding. Even snobs, and especially very
young snobs, have ideals of a kind.

And now Eton was looming near; we were to go
to Mr. Lowry's house in January, and my parents'

theories about home education would be put to the
test. My brother and I were all agog, and expected to
take Remove, and to win a half-crown bet with Mr.
Jack Smith. (He must have had, I think, a tip from his
brother, Mr. Francis, who had seen us do a trial at Les
Mayens.) We knew a great deal about Eton. We
knew by heart that minor classic *A Day of my Life at
Eton*, and my father had sent for the current School
List, so that we might learn the names of the boys at
Lowry's house. What had we missed by not going to
a private school? Chiefly a grounding in Latin and
Greek grammar, and in the irregular verbs. That loss,
as it turned out, could never be caught up with. I was
taught Greek and Latin for nearly seven years at Eton
and, to my life-long regret, never succeeded in learning
either of them. I cannot read Horace or Catullus with
my feet on the fender, or even upon the radiator; I am
stumped by the inscriptions on tombs and tablets; I
am humiliated when I lunch with Sir Ronald Storrs
or dine with Mr. G. M. Young. I never was, but hate
to think I never could have been, a friend of Mr.
Maurice Baring. It has been, for one who enjoys the
company of educated men, a very real deprivation.
But apart from that serious loss, I do not think we
missed very much. We could not play cricket or football, but at Eton one can be a wet-bob, and football
can be learnt at thirteen. We knew no schoolboy
slang, save for a few words picked up from the bold
aunts of the Cecil boys, but slang requires no grounding. We could not, at first, tell boys apart; they
looked, on my first day in Lower Chapel, as alike as
Chinamen or sheep, but that was just a question of
practice. We were naïve and easily taken in, but that

gave innocent amusement to the others, and did not seriously disconcert ourselves.

On the credit side must be placed, first and foremost, our conviction that one went to school to learn things. Among the games played at private schools, at any rate in the late nineties, must be listed the unending game played against the Masters, the game of ducking and evading such scraps of learning as were half-heartedly aimed at empty heads. Of this game we knew nothing, and our well-drilled consciences, together with, I suppose, the habit of hearing 'rational conversation' (although my father's favourite complaint was of our total incapacity for any such thing), did prevent us from picking up the rules of that game, and from playing it. Not till I was in Sixth Form did I use a crib, or fail to prepare a lesson. And even then it was not to evade the benefit of Dr. Warre's Sunday Questions, but because I was convinced that no conceivable benefit could accrue from answering them, that I relied entirely upon a friend for solving these abstruse and irrelevant conundrums. (It was a weekly bitterness to him that the results of his labours, dished up by me in different words, invariably scored higher marks than as served up by himself, without sauce.)

This sounds priggish enough, but I do not think there was conscious priggery in it. We knew that we had been sent to Eton at great expense, and that Eton was a place for learning. Very well, then. I feel pretty sure that it was the collective 'small-boy' sophistication of the private schools that led to the fashionable practice of doing as little work as possible.

Further credits are due to my parents' system. An important one, to me personally, was the exhilaration

of my first half at Eton. The other new boys, while
cheerful enough, saw no particular fun in going into
school, in going into Lower Chapel, in fagging, in being
'an Etonian', in being away from home, independent,
a self-contained unit, 'Jones minor.' I revelled in it all,
day by day, almost hour by hour. It is certain that my
parents' plan had not been directed towards emancipat-
ing us from our totalitarian home. Rather, I suspect,
we were to be missionaries, spreading its sweet influ-
ences. But, in the event, there is no doubt that the
impact of Eton upon a new boy straight from home
was, in contrast to that felt by a boy from a 'prep'
school, entirely delectable. And the credit, although
unplanned, must be given to the system.

Minor credits were our facility in French, our bow-
ing acquaintance with the poetry of Tennyson, Browning, and Matthew Arnold (which counterbalanced with
some of the Masters, if with none of the boys, our
complete ignorance of the names of great cricketers),
and a ready-made belief, not far from mystical, in the
high privilege of being Eton boys. We came to Eton
as her lovers; the others trailed cloudlets of Ludgrove
glory, and fell in love later. They missed the young-
eyed, self-forgetting rush to meet Romance.

So then, in January 1898, we went back to England
with our parents and had our hair cut, for the first time
in our lives, to the shortness suitable for manly English
schoolboys. And that was not all. Cranmer was for
a few weeks without a tenant and we picnicked there
for a few nights, mainly that we, Norfolk bred, might
not have to face the great world in the vulnerable state
of never having fired a gun or killed a rabbit. Each in
turn went off to the woods with Taylor and a 12-bore;

each in turn killed his rabbits, first sitting, then running. It was good to be alive that winter morning, in the old Square Wood, and to see the rabbit turn head over heels, stone dead, and to sniff the little wisps of smoke that oozed from the breech as I broke the gun to reload. We might not have heard of Palairet or Spooner, but we had hung over our beds the masks of fox and hare, and we had killed our ground-game, with no toy 20-bore, but with a grown man's weapon. We were greatly strengthened.

My parents took us down to Eton and said goodbye, on a winter's night, at the door of a third-class carriage on Windsor station. And then we turned and walked down Windsor hill, hands in pockets, to 'm'tutor's'. And I remember to this day the happiness that warmed my heart, the sense of liberation, the joyful expectancy, of which it would have been indecorous to speak, even to my brother, but which found expression, I feel sure, in a slight backward tilting of my new top-hat, an irrepressible springiness in my gait. It was a very jaunty Jones minor that went tripping down to Eton beneath the gas-lamps.

CHAPTER III

ETON

I DID not sleep my first night at Lowry's. It was partly, no doubt, exhilaration that kept me awake, but it was also due to the self-flushing apparatus in Mr. Lowry's 'rears'. The sudden, rushing flow of water, followed by long drawn-out gurgles, came at intervals of about ten minutes all through the night. So far, not more than four or five new boys had arrived, and I could only account for this extraordinary night-long frequency of plug-pulling by some dire epidemic among the other new boys or in Mr. Lowry's household. I was much concerned, and greatly relieved next morning to hear that nobody had been poisoned, and to discover the simple, beneficent cause of my 'nuit blanche'. But who wants to sleep their first night as an Etonian? We sat for our examination with confidence and relish. These were the good, easy days before the Common Entrance examination, or indeed any entrance examination at all. Mr. Francis had been trying to frighten us at Les Mayens. You were accepted for Eton in the week, if not on the day, of your birth, when your father sent a telegram to some Master likely to have a House in thirteen years' time. The examination was to decide, not your entrance, but your form. If it proved that you knew nothing at all, you were sent to throw ink-bottles at your peers in Third Form under

Bunny Hare. If at fifteen, heavy, spotty, and in tails, you were still unfit for the Upper School, you were 'superannuated', and lost to sight until you turned up fifty years later as a distinguished General or Colonial Governor. After two days of writing ('on one side of the paper only') in Upper School, that great glorious room of Wren's that made one small boy at any rate almost too proud to concentrate, a list appeared in Ingalton-Drake's window. Jones ma. and Jones mi. were placed, next to one another, in Middle Fourth. We were sorry for my father, but far too happy to be sorry for ourselves.

There was one more formality before we new boys were absorbed into the School at large. The Headmaster, Dr. Warre, addressed us. It was in Upper School. The occasion was, for us, tremendous. There he stood, waiting, this great square man, with a broad silk band round his middle, gazing at a high window, and chewing the inside of his cheek, as was his habit. He looked all justice and authority. 'Come up here, boys, don't be afraid.' An enormous voice rumbled from the depths of him. And then he spoke to us, paternally, dropping his final G's, moving his strong lips as one does to a lip-reader, now in a vibrant bass, now in a sudden tenor. He spoke of our responsibility as Etonians; he was encouraging and kind. Then, out of the blue, came an astonishing admonition. He told us to beware of 'filth', to avoid even talking 'filth'. I was completely baffled. I knew a great deal about filth, after that summer among the footpaths and bushes of Valais. But here, at Eton? Could he be telling us to look where we trod, because of the occasional dog-mess on the pavements? And who ever wanted to talk about these horrors? I had always been queasy, and it seemed to me to be the most unnecessary, the most surprising of warnings. We were not in Switzerland. I was too much taken aback even to discuss it afterwards with the other new boys. Did they understand? I shall never know. A year or two later, I should have understood him; for it was a commonplace in those days, uncontested by Masters or boys, and a particular obsession of visiting preachers, that sex, although given to us by God, was a dirty little secret. The strongest of human impulses, the most delectable of human enjoyments, was equated, in our hierarchy of values, with ordure.

Charles Lowry, m'tutor, was an old Colleger and a wet-bob, a big bluff man with a heavy black moustache. He had been a School or College friend of my father's, and he was invariably kind and encouraging to us. I was sufficiently unsophisticated to like him steadily throughout the two years before he left Eton to become Headmaster of Tonbridge. I was never infected with the fashion in his house to pretend to be slightly scornful of 'the Man' and his ways. It was true that I never suffered violence at his hands. When, in pupil room, he hurled a Greek Liddell and Scott at Fremantle, a very small 'tug' whose classical tutor he was, and knocked him off his bench, I was glad to have been there to see it. And when he beat Hasluck and Morris over the head with the crib they had been compelled to fetch and surrender, after translating some Greek word as 'a cold collation', I had little sympathy for Hasluck and Morris. I was by that time tolerant of the use of cribs by others, though not (for the 'overdraft's' sake) by myself; but the idiocy of thinking that 'cold collation' could ever

pass muster as a boy's own expression seemed to
deserve a head-beating. And after all, a Kelly's *Key to
the Classics* was not a blunt instrument. It was a small,
blue, sinister little book in paper covers. And to one
who had been up to Mr. Hubert Brinton, that grim,
heroic man who, unknown to us, went through his
daily task suffering agonies from neuritis, m'tutor's
occasional fits of physical violence seemed mild indeed.
I have seen Mr. Brinton, when a boy accidentally
dropped a book, deliberately, with one great scythe-
stroke of his throbbing arm, sweep everything, books,
papers, and ink-bottle, off his own magisterial desk. I
have seen him stride across the room, shouting 'Don't
stare at me, Bardswell, with those great cod's eyes
of yours', and, seizing the astonished Bardswell by
the lapels, haul him across the schoolroom and hurl
him down the stairs outside the door. He was right
about the cod's eyes, but how could this violence,
we wondered, diminish their natural protuberance?
'Briny' was a holy terror in division; but his House
loved him dearly and, from all I have been told,
deservedly.

Middle Fourth was taken by Mr. Mount, in one of
the low, ancient chambers from whose latticed windows
one looks out upon Schoolyard and the tall buttresses of
Chapel. It was dark; the Master's view of the boys
was interrupted by oaken pillars, black with age; the
forms, polished by generations of young bottoms, were
too narrow for ease; the desks, carved with a thousand
names, were too narrow to write upon; it was un-
warmed in winter, airless in summer. No Education
Authority in the land would tolerate Lower School,
but in my eyes it was beyond criticism.

Go into His gates with thankfulness,
And into His courts with praise

we sang twice a year in Chapel, when Mr. A. C. Ainger's
Hymn on the special paper was given out. During
my first half at Eton, at half-past seven on winter
mornings, shivering in that least protective clothing in
the world, an Eton jacket, I went into Mr. Mount's
bleak and gas-lit schoolroom with thankfulness and
with praise. The new boys from 'my last school' did
not. They did, however, jostle and crowd, 'after
twelve,' round the window of the adjoining schoolroom. This was the Lower Master's room, where he
taught Upper Fourth, and if you were not too short,
and could use your elbows and were prepared to risk
your top-hat, you might get a glimpse of the block,
and the victim's pink behind, and the swing of the
birch-rod in the heavy, purposeful hand of 'the Flea'.

Mr. Mount was a grave young master with a high
white forehead and an air of having stepped down
from a stained-glass window, who was to die, like my
brother, before that year was out. He encouraged us
to draw and paint the subjects of our lessons, classical
or historical or biblical. It was not difficult to introduce
Lisa's boats and square-shouldered boatmen into these
pictures, and my brother and I soon found our paintings pinned upon one of the black pillars, with 'very
good' scrawled across one corner. As the drawings
were unsigned, we felt it to be only due to ourselves
to inform the other boys, as they crowded round the
pillar, of the identity of the artists. Any form of 'side'
was taboo; and we had a swift lesson, by the scarifying
and contemptuous comments of the crowd, on the
wisdom of not blowing your own trumpet. We took

L

it to heart and soon became as proficient as the rest in
that endearing British false modesty which, skilfully
used, can win so many games of tennis, so many rubbers
of bridge.

What we learnt in school that first half I do not
remember, although I do recall that our first saying-
lesson began 'Aspera robigo, parcas cerealibus herbis'.
Saying-lessons, although learnt by rote, since that was
easier than to hunt up 'robigo' in the dictionary, were
little trouble to us, for we had learnt by heart since
the days of Miss Margaret Wood's *First Poetry Book*.
'Parsing', for which special paper had to be bought
from the Little Man in Ingalton-Drake's, was new to
us, but we were conscientious and attentive, and in
Trials Jones ma. won the Trials Prize and the Brinckman
Divinity Prize, and Jones mi. was second. That meant
a 'double' into Remove, and my father, delighted,
took all the credit. But what we learnt out of school
was much and various.

At m'tutor's we were regarded as freaks, and much
frequented by the other Lower boys, who enjoyed test-
ing our boundless credulity as much as teaching us,
fraternally, the ropes. They were a kindly lot, Browning and Llewellyn and Edwards minor, but never ceased
to wonder at our enjoyment of such things as fagging.
For myself, my heart leapt up when Cockerell, who
rowed in the Eight and was in 'Pop', told me after
prayers to put a can of water in his bath, or sent me
with a note to his friend George Lloyd. To be free, if
only as a valet, of Cockerell's room, where the Rules
of the Eton Society were framed in light-blue ribbon,
and the white cap of the Eight hung upon the corner of
a picture, was to taste privilege indeed. If ever a boy

was made for hero-worship it was Sam Cockerell, with
his good looks, his warm, male voice, his kind heart
and fine manners. Predestined, through an inherited
incapacity for ball games, to be a wet-bob, I decided,
after one upward glance at Cockerell, to row in the
Eight. In a week or two I had seen, arm-in-arm with
a row of 'Pops', in his reefer-jacket with gold buttons,
the Captain of the Boats himself. Waldorf Astor's
bearing surprised me a little by its modesty. He did
not quite carry himself as I meant to carry myself. For
my mind was now made up, my ambition settled.
When my father had described the Captain of the
Boats in his own day as 'the greatest swell on earth', I
had not, for all my consciousness of having been born
to command, considered this particular pinnacle as
mine; but to hear of grandeur is one thing, to see it is
another. Six years later, wearing that reefer-jacket, it
was the legendary figure of my father's memories, not
the modest dignity of Waldorf Astor, that I tried, not
unsuccessfully, I fear, to ape.

My father's views about 'liturgical traps' were not,
and are not, current at Eton. We went to Chapel every
day, and twice on Sundays. Since this was Eton's law,
it was acceptable to me, but I am not quite sure that I
identified the God who looked down upon those rows
of kneeling boys and wanted them to be pure with
the God who sat above the sunlit hills of Valescure
and wanted us to be kind. Although the Masters in
Desk, and the Lower Master himself, the redoubtable
'Flea', knelt with us, it was a boy's God whom we
were expected to worship, a God who, in the words
used every night by Mr. Lowry at house-prayers, 'was
about our path and about our bed, and spied out all

our ways'. In spite of this espionage, we remained care-free and praised the Spy at the top of our lungs, if the tune was a good one. Twice a Half we were told to remain in our seats after the Blessing, and Dr. Lloyd, he who struggled with the bird within him, came twittering in, and tripped up and down the length of Lower Chapel, teaching us how to 'point' the Psalms. 'Following the ewes / great with lambs' he sang in a high and husky falsetto, for we were a chapelful of trebles, and he tried bravely to encompass the notes written for us. We enjoyed these practices, for the time was taken off the next school, and Dr. Lloyd, whole-hearted for the music and faintly rollicking, somehow took the holiness out of the Psalms and made them human and enjoyable. Give small boys plenty of singing, and they will go happily to church; but holiness scares them.

For myself, as a new boy, Lower Chapel had a fascination which had nothing to do with the service. Here, for the first time in my life, I could sit quietly and study the faces of hundreds of boys. Milling about the Crimean cannon at Absence, or outside the school-room door, they looked to me, as I have said, all alike; but in Chapel they were comparatively still, their top-hats were piled upon the broad window-ledges in the Ante-Chapel, and there was a plan of seating arrangements by which they could be identified. I was astounded at the variety, and still more at the maturity in their countenances. I was particularly fascinated by a thick-set boy in the front row opposite to me. His name was Melles, and, in my eyes, he looked about forty. He had a weathered, sleepy old country face, with wrinkles at the corners of his eyes, and an air of

great experience. He was actually fourteen. How did
he look to his mother, I wonder? Then there was
Nugent, the complete weasel, thin, predatory, entirely
un-boyish, and Barclay minor, hunched and haggard,
with weary eyelids, who looked as if all the world's
burdens were upon his thin shoulders. Very different
was Barclay major. This enormous young man, with
his even taller friend Marsham, and Cookson who was
reputed to shave every morning, led a devil-may-care
group known to us as Lower Boy Pop. When Marsham swung from the cross-bars of the lampposts going
up Keate's Lane, we believed them to be 'capables de
tout'. If Eton had her Flashman, Barclay major, I
thought, must be he. I regarded him, with his long,
thin neck and his longer tail-coat, with shrinking and
suspicion. Seventeen years later, when the Rev. Hum-
phrey Barclay was Padre to the 9th Cavalry Brigade in
France, I was fortunate to come to know the most
tender-hearted of men, who, if he ever had to contend
with the Old Adam, can have met him in no more
sinister shape than that of the Old Horse-Coper. So
much for a small boy's skill in judging character.

'Daddy' Lloyd, whose small golden beard seemed
to us a badge of his calling, was the precentor and
organist in Upper Chapel. Sixth Form Collegers and
Mr. S. G. Lubbock were accustomed, to our wonder,
to linger in the Ante-Chapel after the service was over,
in order to hear Daddy Lloyd complete his playing of
the Bach fugues chosen for the Voluntary. Why was
it the Collegers, the boys with brains, who lingered?
Must you have brains for Bach? He seems to me to
stir the solar plexus as much as the skull. However
that may be, they lingered and listened, and I am sorry

that I did not do the same. As Secretary of the Musical Society, I could have incurred no suspicions by doing so.

The Eton Musical Society was Daddy Lloyd's main preoccupation outside his duties as precentor. While sitting for our examination, we new boys had been beckoned, one by one, into another room, where Dr. Lloyd sat at an upright piano. He struck a note: 'Sing that.' If we hit it, he took down our names and told us that we should be members of the Musical Society. My brother and I both hit it. We joined the Musical Society, and I never abandoned it. I owed to it an enormous amount of pleasure, and some moments of the most acute misery I suffered while at Eton. The pleasure was never sweeter than during my first Half. I had not heard choral singing, or an orchestra (save that one night in Geneva) in all my life, and I came away from the weekly practices in the Music Schools full of new stirrings and vague longings. It was fun to sit high up in the lofty amphitheatre among the trebles, and to see the 'Pops' come in, with button-holes and silk house-colour scarves, to seat themselves familiarly with the singing 'beaks', tenor with tenor, bass with bass. But when the words and music of 'Alexander's Feast' began to take shape for me, I felt a new and strange elation. 'Thay-ay-is led ther-er-er-er way' sang a single choirboy, in the rising and falling Handelian phrase, and I was in ecstasy. 'The lovely Thais by his side' — Lisa had worn a Greek dress as Galatea and I saw again, on Thais, the straight, thin folds that had fallen from the brooch on Lisa's shoulder. Music was getting mixed up with lovely woman. And 'none but the brave deserve the fair'. I had never before considered the question of deserving the fair: Handel and Dryden together made it seem urgent and actual. And when a full manly bass — was it 'Thunderguts' of Upper Chapel Choir? — sang that war was toil and trouble, honour but an empty bubble, I despised our piping trebles, and feared that lovely Thais would have eyes and ears for none but 'Thunderguts'. But I forgot even Thais and my own inadequacy in her starry eyes when Handel's poignant semitones bewailed Darius great and good, by too severe a fate fallen, fallen, fallen, fallen, fallen from his high estate, and lying, weltering in his blood, alone on the bare earth. Handel, out to stir up all moods, soft and ferocious, by turns, brought it off, with one small boy, to perfection. I went back to m'tutor's through the fog moved and exalted, and avid for next week's practice.

The moments of acute misery came later. At the School Concert it was *de rigueur* for performers and audience alike to wear full evening dress. We had never possessed any such thing. My mother's idea about our clothes had never been conventional, and we had been accustomed to change, in the evenings, into white flannels. At my first Concert, since I was still in jackets, there was no major crisis, as I was able to borrow a low waistcoat from another Lower boy; even so, Browning's incredulous horror at hearing that we did not possess evening trousers or waistcoats made me feel a qualm of social inferiority. But when, in subsequent years, an evening tail-coat was required, I was obliged, amid much jeering, to hire the whole outfit from Denman and Goddard. The jeering was hard to bear, but the contemptuous surprise on the face of the man at Denman and Goddard was far worse. He supposed it could be managed, and it was managed; but at what a cost of suffering! Not until I was eighteen, when my father put me on my allowance, did I possess a dress suit of my own. It cost four guineas. There had been a wild moment of hope earlier on, when I was fourteen. I was on long leave in London, and we were to go to *The Gondoliers*. My father suddenly announced that I must have evening clothes. He took me to 'Our Boys' in Oxford Street. A dress suit was produced. My heart leapt within me. My father waved the suit aside. 'A boy like him only needs a dinner-jacket.' And a dinner-jacket it was, completely useless to me, in fact a disaster, for its possession barred all further possibility of raising the question of evening clothes for years to come. I had a dinner-jacket, all a boy needed. It may seem extraordinary that, suffering so absurdly as I did from the recurrent agonies of hiring, I never told my father about the School Concerts. But in these years the 'poverty' and the overdraft, and my father's reputed sleepless nights from worrying, made any request for money or expenditure absolutely out of the question, so far as I was concerned. It was a question of conscience. I know now that had I confessed to my misery I should have been given a dress-suit out of hand. But how could one go to a ruined man with a plea that would cost money to satisfy? It couldn't be done, any more than one could tell him that ten shillings a Half, even for a Lower boy, was very short commons indeed.

Before leaving the Eton Musical Society I must explain that the fact that I became Secretary of it, entitled by custom to a special round of applause as I mounted the stage at the School Concerts, had nothing to do with any musicianship in myself. I was as wholly

unmusical then as I have since remained, alas, in spite
of experiencing, in listening to music, one of the major
pleasures of life. The Secretary of the Musical Society
was appointed on the same principle whereby retired
Field-Marshals or Colonial Governors join the boards
of Big Business of which they know nothing. I was a
'good name' in the eyes of the public. Small boys, as
Dr. Lloyd pointed out to me, could not pretend that
the Musical Society was cultured or aesthetic, if it had
a beefy oarsman as Secretary. I was there as a bait to
the Philistines. (On the same very British principle I
was promoted to Colour-Sergeant in the Corps, in
spite of a career of utter slackness and indifference, and
even hard pressed by the C.O., Colonel Somerville,
to take a commission. This I resisted. 'But why?'
'Because it means lunching with the Masters on field-
days, Sir.' He winced, poor man, but did not pursue
the subject.)

Looking back to the short days of that Winter Half,
I find that passages obsess my memory. Passages,
narrow and wainscoted, down which we raced to the
call of 'Lower boy!'; passages where we lingered and
gossiped in front of notice-boards; passages sweating
with moisture after a game of passage-football; the
complicated passages of other Houses, through which
one had to find a way, when Praepostor, to the Dame's
room. For even a new boy had his week of office as
Praepostor, when it was his business to mark in the
Praepostor's Book the names of boys absent from
Division or from Chapel, and to collect an 'excuse' for
them from their Dame. The massive new Houses had
not then been built, and we lived, for the most part, in
intricate rabbit-warrens. When an epidemic of measles

or mumps broke out, a dozen boys might be absent at one time, and a small Praepostor, wandering to 'W.D.'s' down Judy's passage, and thence to Donaldson's at the far end of Cow Lane, had sometimes to skip his breakfast. It was a bad system, now long abolished, but I loved my week of office. It was the sort of thing that could be tolerated at Eton, and only at Eton. And is there, perhaps, a taint of Original Jack-in-Office in all of us? May only the French enjoy being functionaries? I suspect, from the satisfaction I felt as I made my rounds with my long, narrow book, that I had the makings, never yet given a chance to develop, of a successful small-town Mayor.

My brother and I duly caught the measles, an event not worth recording had it not marked a definite step in the process of moulding us to a common pattern. For measles ended in sick leave, and to go on sick leave, to my grandmother at Camberley, we had to put on our 'change-clothes'. We had arrived at Eton in tails and Eton jacket respectively, and until the morning of going on sick leave no boy in the house knew, or could have suspected, the dreadful truth that our 'change-clothes', lying hid at the bottom of our ottomans, included knickerbockers. When we suddenly appeared, cheerful and unafraid, in our home-spun knickerbockers, the shock to Lowry's House was great. We, who had been amiable freaks, were in real danger of becoming 'touts', not merely eccentric but socially 'not quite, quite'. We were, in the event, forgiven, but we had had a fright, and I was thenceforward closely concerned with conformity to accepted standards. The measles thus left their mark, not on our bodies, but upon our souls. My brother explained, in the holidays, that knickerbockers were not the thing, and my mother saw to it that my father told us each to order a pair of trousers that should match, as near as might be, our coats and waistcoats. That they did not really match was of course spotted, and the cause of adverse comment. I can remember thinking that happiness — true peace of mind — could be mine if only my change-trousers could match my change-coat. I had to wait some years for that blessed marriage of twin-tweeds, and for the inward repose it brought me.

It might be thought that this pressure to conform, continuous until my last two years at Eton brought the freedom of 'Pop', would have damped my satisfaction in being liberated from that other pressure to conform, at home, with my mother's exacting standards of behaviour, taste, and affections. But it was not so. The pressure at home had been upon head and heart; one had to think, and to love, to order. At Eton you could think and love what you liked: only in external matters, in clothes, or in deportment, need you do as others did. Such conformity would have cost me nothing had I been insensible enough to beg that a few more pounds be added to the heavy expense of keeping a boy at Eton.

None the less I feel sure that the continuous squeezing of boys into identical moulds which was part of Public School life at the turn of the century was a bad thing. I was lucky, since in my case Balliol broke the mould once and for all; but not every boy could go to Balliol, or even to a University; and anything that deprives society of diversity in its members diminishes its quality. I believe things are better nowadays. But the urge in boys to be like everybody else is strong;

and, when they are herded together, an urge which is not easily countered. Yet, even in those days, I believe that Eton, with the separate rooms, the leavening of boys from spacious and original homes, the House-masters of character, the beauty and dignity of herself, was kinder and less discouraging to 'freaks', and to boys who could not make their mark in games, than any other school.

Our holidays at Valescure, thanks to the Trials results and the reports, were mildly triumphant. My father, who had forgotten Mr. Meneer and the Eton Latin Grammar, talked openly to visitors of his success. And soon we were back at Eton, and in Lower Remove, and the chestnut-tree by the New Schools was in blossom, and the playing-fields smelt of new-mown grass, and the sound of bat on ball came, clicking of summer, from the nets on Upper Sixpenny. We could not go on the river until we had passed in swimming, and the water at Cuckoo Weir was still too cold for that; so, sharing one enormous old bat from the Cranmer attics, we went, without pads or gloves, to be 'picked up' in a 'refuse' game. We had never before played in a game of what we thought of as 'double wicket'. We did not know what an 'over' was, or the names of the fielders' positions. We could not field or catch or throw. In these games the next-man-in had to go out onto the field and umpire. We neither knew where to stand nor what to look for. Kind-hearted Browning did his best to instruct us 'cuckoos', as he called us, and, being declared wet-bobs, we were the objects of amusement rather than jeering. I managed to enjoy even a refuse-game. After all, it was all part of Eton.

Hugh Macnaghten took Lower Remove. This uncommon, ardent man, sentimental minor poet and half-
saint, knew how to teach small boys. When construing an Ode of Horace, and listening to Macnaghten's
vivid talk about Horace at Baiae, and of what his
friends probably gave him to eat at their dinner-parties,
we knew that, next day, we should be recapitulating
the Ode itself and the talk round about it in a game of
'cricket'. This was played as follows: Macnaghten
named two boys as Captains of the opposing sides. The
Captains then 'picked' their teams. And, for once,
those boys who, like the spectacled Sandilands or the
omniscient Raymond Parr, were picked last in the
playing-fields, found themselves being snapped up first.
After tossing for innings, the Captains put in a boy to
bowl and bat respectively. The bowler asked a question relating to yesterday's lesson. If the bat could
answer to Macnaghten's satisfaction, he scored a run.
If not, he was out. Next man in. If the runs came too
fast, a new bowler was tried. Even the dullest boys
were keen to make runs or to take a wicket, and there
is no question but that Macnaghten had hit upon a
most effective dodge for concentrating our attention.
I have an idea that, had I remained in Lower Remove
for the next six years, I might have learned Latin and
Greek.

The sun cannot really have shone every day during
that Summer Half, dappling the stone-capped wall
where the 'Pops' sat in their white waistcoats, because
'passing' was put off again and again owing to the cold.
But at last the day came when 'W.D.', looking like
Mr. Punch with the jokes left out, sat in a punt at
Cuckoo Weir and called upon us, naked and shivering,

to dive from another punt and swim round the rye-peck. The shock of the cold water, after our warm Mediterranean, all but deprived me of the capacity to swim; however, thanks to m'tutor being W.D.'s assessor, I gasped and spluttered through to a narrow 'pass'. After that, goodbye to the refuse games. My brother and I hired a 'perfect'; Mr. Jenkins' teaching in the adapted punt on the Wensum had not been wasted: we were pertinacious in begging m'tutor's senior wet-bobs to give us sporadic half-hours of coaching, and in the end Jones ma. and Jones mi., coxed by Queen Victoria's grandson, the diminutive Duke of Albany, rowed their way into the Final of the Lower Boy Pulling. In the Final we came in fourth and last; it was won by two boys with heavy black moustaches and hairy forearms, but to be there at all won us a mention in Cockerell's speech at the House Supper. People who have not received a mention in a speech by Cockerell cannot be expected to understand the intense inward elation that it caused. We were clapped; we tasted glory. Yet, looking back over the years to that first Summer Half, it is not the river, or the Lower Boy Pulling, or Hugh Macnaghten's wayward dealings with us, now hearty, now shyly withdrawn, that I see most clearly. It is a picture, precise in the sunshine, of Jones minor coming back up Keate's Lane from Lower Chapel on the morning of the Fourth of June. He is wearing a button-hole; he has just been singing 'Now thank we all our God' with immense and genuine fervour; he is walking in a kind of intoxication. For everything that goes to the making of Eton, the mellow red bricks, the elms, the river and the playing-fields, the traditions, the community, the high privilege of belonging to it, had suddenly coalesced into a single flash of delight. It was a mystic moment for a Thomas Traherne, not for him, to describe. But it left a mark; and I cannot help thinking that a School which could visit with such a benediction a not very imaginative boy of thirteen must possess a singular grace. At all events it was in Keate's Lane beneath the window-boxes, and not at Harrow, that the vision was vouchsafed.

We began the summer holidays as guests, with our parents, at Didlington Hall, the Norfolk home of the Valescure aunts. In a week my elder brother was dead of pneumonia. I had already, as I have told, suffered the extreme, the ultimate pain of bereavement. This was somehow different. I was frightened. I was frightened because my mother did not cry, because her voice changed, becoming hoarse and level and expressionless; because she spent the morning of my brother's death not in seclusion, but walking rapidly up and down the great Didlington terraces with the specialist from London who had been staying for two nights in the house. A man she hardly knew! She was asking for reassurance, I learned long afterwards, not only that nothing had been left undone, but that human personality survives death. He gave her the first; he could not give her the second. Her conventional, Christian faith failed her altogether. Her mainspring, which had been our mainspring, was broken. Dry-eyed, inwardly despairing, she neglected, from the first hour, no single detail of her daily routine in managing and directing our lives. Only she became infinitely gentle; there was no more checking or fault-finding; we never again had to live up to standards a little above our natural capacities. She abdicated, from the day my brother

died, from her austere rulership, and when, by good
fortune, her faith and high spirits eventually returned
to her, she became, for me at least, the most trusted
confidant, the most beloved of friends. The blow must
have been bitter indeed to my father and mother. My
brother had everything that delights parental hearts:
great good looks, strength, eagerness, intelligence, affection, and conscience. He was the eldest son, in days
when the heir was the heir. He was irreplaceable.
Plain, snub, undemonstrative, I had no qualifications for
taking his place. My parents did not share my secret
that I was born to command, and I do not think they
suspected that my brother, always the leader in physical
adventures, was my follower in our imaginative lives.
But my mother's grief was sharpened by remorse. Her
very pride in her eldest son had led her to watch and
check and discipline him with especial rigour. He
could be at times, not exactly rough, but boisterous, to
a degree which crossed the boundaries of sweetness and
light. And now she could neither revoke, nor explain,
a strictness which haunted and tormented her.

The fright and shock which I felt at seeing my
mother change at a blow from a high-spirited leader to
a passive, expressionless provider distracted me from
my own bereavement. And my overpowering need
for a special object of affection threw me, within forty-
eight hours, round the neck of my younger brother,
hitherto a mere hanger-on of us older ones. I adopted
him, almost fiercely, as my new 'buddy', unaware of
what it would cost me in future disquietude. For there
was to be no Eton for him; he was at a private school
which he hated, and then at a crammer's which he
hated only a little less, and I suffered many pangs on his

account, comparing his wretched lot with my fair one.
After passing out of the *Britannia* he went for a two years'
voyage in H.M.S. *Flora*. His going was a third bereavement which cut deep, and I had the shock of seeing, in
the Eton High Street, a newspaper poster announcing
'Wreck of H.M.S. *Flora*'. Physically sick, I bought the
paper—to find that the ship was merely aground off
Esquimault, with no lives lost. But I had thereafter,
for many years, an anxiety-neurosis, nourished on
London posters: 'Torpedo boat cut in halves' when he
was in Torpedo boats; 'Submarine sunk, loss of all
lives' when he was in Submarines. There had been no
war in those days to make anxiety the common lot of
us all, and I was defenceless against its recurrent, dis-
abling assaults. One sees a sailor so seldom that it is,
on a cool view, a mistake to be fond of one. In my
hour of necessity, however, he came, unawares, to my
rescue; and my father, on a happy impulse, bought me
a Kodak and an apparatus for developing my own
plates. It is curious to reflect that a Kodak could play
any real part in solacing a boy of thirteen for the loss
of the hourly companion, day and night, of his whole
life, the object of his concentrated affection. But boys
live, not in the past, but from minute to minute, and
this new interest and activity did, in fact, comfort me
enormously.

My father, whose home has always been in the passing hour, also recovered his appetite for living therein
in a surprisingly short time. His resilience enabled us
to believe that in time my mother, too, would recover;
we did not then understand that she had lost, not only
a child, but her faith.

In the first days of my fright and dismay I had a

M

special dread of returning to Eton alone. I could not see a Jones minor there without his major; I shrunk from questions, from condolences, from a confused prevision of fresh pangs and embarrassments. My parents promised that I should not return to Eton till after Christmas. By the end of the summer holiday, spent on photography, I should have been ready to go back to school, but I dared not say so. How could I go after so few weeks and tell my mother that my grief had abated? It could not be done; and a plan was made for me to go to Paris, to learn French in the family of Madame Poulain, while my elder sister stayed with the family of Georges Deloche.

My father took us to Dover to see us off, but bought a newspaper there which made him change his mind. For the excitement over Marchand's flag planted in the sands at Fashoda was at its height, and war with France appeared, for a day or two, not merely possible but probable. So the boat sailed without us, and we found ourselves in a crowd lining the Dover streets to watch a square, brick-red man with heavy moustaches and a bowler hat too small for him, walk, in a tweed suit, to some civic reception. It was the Sirdar, fresh from the Battle of Omdurman, and likely soon, if my father's newspaper was right, to be fighting a second Waterloo. We cheered him on both accounts.

A day or so later my father scoffed at the idea of war and sent us to Paris. Monsieur and Madame Poulain lived in a stuffy, dark, overfurnished flat somewhere near the Arc-de-Triomphe. He was bald and bearded and went daily to his bureau; she was prim and depressed and sighed a great deal. I made a gaffe straight away by asking her what Monsieur Poulain did at his bureau. She replied that he was in business. 'But what business?' Her answer was that it was not for a little boy like me to ask questions; that if I thought that because some people did not live in a château with a park and many servants they were of less value than those who did, I was greatly mistaken; that people must be judged by what they were, not by what they possessed, and so on. It was a surprising answer to a simple question, and even my unsophisticated mind concluded at once that Monsieur Poulain's position at the bureau was one of which Madame Poulain was ashamed.

I had a very dull time. Madame Poulain sighed even when playing cribbage. She dutifully took my sister and myself to museums and galleries; but we were too young for such things without guidance, and Madame Poulain sat on a bench while we wandered, bored and at sea, among the objects of art. The one relief to my dullness was an occasional outing with Robert, the Poulains' grown-up son. Robert was vivacious and good-looking but, although he lived in the flat, he was rarely seen by me, for he went off early and came home late. But Madame Poulain distrusted him; 'Voyons, Robert, faut pas dire des saletés devant Lawrie'. It was as surprising as Dr. Warre's address; I had never heard Robert say a word about filth; on the contrary, he generally talked about ladies. There was one very beautiful lady indeed who had come to discuss a charity bazaar, and had afterwards sung at an evening party. She was tall and very slim and had great eyes and beautiful clothes and I was very much taken with her — she belonged, somehow, to the music of *Alexander's Feast*. So when, after the soirée, her looks were discussed at the Poulain dinner-table, and Robert, while admitting that she had a lovely face, added, with a sweep of his palm across his upper waistcoat, 'mais elle a le sein trop plat,' I was dumbfounded at Madame Poulain's: 'Pas de saletés, Robert!' How could flatness be associated with 'saleté?' In fairness to the French people, it must be said that Madame Poulain had been, before her marriage, either British or half-British, and so wholly or partly inhibited, by heredity, from accepting her Creator's handiwork without disgust.

I do not think that I gained anything from this dismal interlude, except an improvement in my French accent which did me no good with my fellows at Eton, although I resisted the temptation of affecting a British accent in order to please them. I refused to pronounce 'avez' to rhyme with 'de Havvy', as did the others (and as did, according to his own account, Monseigneur Ronald Knox when, on holiday in France and suddenly asked to take Confessions in the place of a sick priest, he could think of no better reply to a frail, perfumed, and penitent adulteress than 'Oh voos avvy, avvy voo?'). It was rather a delicate matter on occasions during the hour of 'Classical French', which at Eton does not mean the French Classics, but French taught by a Classics Master. For in addition to the regular weekly French lesson with M. Hua or M. Cuvelier, one school-time a week was allocated to reading a book, generally by Erckmann-Chatrian, with our Form-master. And our form-master's accent was not seldom in the 'Boulong, Toulong, le Continong' class. But I stuck to my guns, and resented being called a 'Frenchy' as much as I had during my first week resented the word 'slacker'

applied to my father when, in reply to a question as
to what he did, I had truthfully answered that he did
nothing. The question and the reception given to my
answer dispose, incidentally, of the accusation that
Eton at the turn of the century was a school for the
sons of 'the idle rich'.

Nobody changed their clothes before dinner at
Madame Poulain's, and the bath was only available on
certain days; and I, who had hitherto known but three
classes of persons, gentlemen, shopkeepers, and work-
ing-people, began to suspect that there might be degrees
of gentility. Had Madame Poulain been French by
birth, no suspicion would have arisen, since I did not
expect to find foreigners as clean in their habits as we
were; but I could not place her, in her English girlhood, in any surroundings such as I had so far known.
She did not read books, or like fresh air, or have flowers
in her rooms. She was formal with her rare visitors,
and they were formal with her; everybody was dull,
and respectful, and on their guard. I became bored and
critical, and could easily, had my sojourn in that
stuffy flat been prolonged, have picked up the germ of
snobbery. Fortunately it was not prolonged; I joined
my family at Valescure, where my father had the
distraction of building a villa, and after Christmas I
returned, in tails, to Eton.

M'tutor had somehow wangled it that I should be
jumped two removes into Lower Division. I was now
an Upper boy, although compelled, by tradition, to be
a fag for a third half. Sixth Form was no longer beyond
my reach. And for the next five years Eton became
for me, increasingly as time went on, not my school
but my life. The holidays, now happy and relaxed

since my mother had abandoned discipline for indulgence, were none the less mere interludes in the serious business of living. I went back to Eton at the beginning of each Half with exhilaration; in that busy and diverse community, in that ancient and numinous place, were centred all my ambition and all my preoccupations.

It would be tiresome any longer to try to record my recollections of Eton in chronological order. I shall attempt, instead, to recall the Masters, and the boys, and the teaching, and the religion, and the habits of mind, and the social pressures which combined to mould an Eton boy in the opening years of the present century. But I shall try, as hitherto, to distinguish clearly between the Eton in which I lived with such zest and the Eton I see, and judge, from a distance of well over fifty years.

Dr. Warre, as we saw him, was greatness itself. I do not think it would be possible to exaggerate the prestige he had with us boys. Even today, I cannot imagine myself a contemporary of Warre's, someone who could call him 'Edmond', pat him on the back, chaff him about his school-mastery ways, pretend to think that he was Headmaster of Harrow. There must, surely, have been such friends in his life, for he was warm-hearted, affectionate, and entirely without pomposity. But no, Imagination refuses to contemplate such persons. Warre stood alone; solitary in his majesty. His physical presence, when he swept into a classroom on one of his periodical visitations, was overpowering; even a tough character like Mr. Impey, all sang-froid and disdain, became pliant and courtier-like when the Head came striding in, and Mr. Dyer ceased, temporarily, to exist. Warre's face was not like other men's faces. The features were absolutely regular; square forehead, straight wooden nose, strong cleft chin, carven lips, straight brows; nothing loose or sagging or pale or mottled; a warm, weathered brown colour over all; whiskers, inclined to be reddish, tickling the broad white tie under his chin. The scale of his face, as of his girth, his feet, his hands, was a little over life-size. His voice could rumble deep down in his belly, or it could soar to a high, tenor note. He strode. There was a story that his top-hat, being refurbished by Solomon at New and Lingwood's, had been tried on and worn by two Lower boys at once.

It is a proof of the strength of an institution that we can afford to laugh at it. Only very devout Catholics make jokes about the Holy Father, and the loyalest hearts enjoyed stories against Queen Victoria, but were uneasy when King Edward VII was spoken of with disrespect. Our pride in, and our reverence for, our great Headmaster did not inhibit us from attempting to mimic him. 'Dere's an evil elephant come into de school. Nobody saw it come in. It came in bit by bit. But we must stamp on it, and destroy it. It's de elephant of bettin' and gamblin'.' Could he have said 'elephant'? I was there; I have sworn to it many times. But he did sometimes mumble. Was it 'element'? For us it was 'elephant', and he remained as great as ever. Indeed, the final test of Warre's simple greatness was its capacity to stand up to, and prevail over, his ineptitude as a teacher. Every boy in Upper School knew that the Head could not preach. In the pulpit he did not even use his great voice. He preached from notes, obscurely, on a text, perhaps, from the Epistle to the Romans. It was theology, unapplied to life, that he gave us in Chapel, without warmth. We had all heard him, on occasions, speak to us from his heart in Upper School, and if his sermons were dull, we blamed St. Paul, not the Head, for that. But only we who had sat under him in Division knew the futility of his teaching. On the subject of triremes he was splendid, animated and enthusiastic, for he was himself a designer of racing eights. But the proper construction of a trireme is a very small back-alley off the broad high road of education; and, with the possible exception of Selwyn K.S. and Macmillan K.S., none of us could follow a word when he read out long passages from Polybius, interspersed with Latin notes, also read aloud. It really seems that Warre believed that Sixth Form boys could understand Greek and Latin as living languages. He set us enormous saying lessons — forty lines at a time from Homer or Virgil, which compelled us to acquire the brain-wrecking knack of memorising for a few hours only. His 'Sunday Questions' teased us with recondite points of scholarship; research, not understanding, won good marks. And for all that, such was the impact upon us of his friendly, manly, generous nature in these intimate sessions, that we remained his devoted adherents, but giving him affection in the place of awe.

Even before I was 'up to' Warre in Sixth Form, when he was still to me the most remote and majestic of figures, I had been given a glimpse of his humanity. It was about five o'clock on a flawless summer morning; my tutor's house had just been burnt down; two little boys, both of them my fags, had died in the flames; and the Headmaster, who had arrived on the scene in pyjamas and a grey woollen dressing-gown, had taken me back with him to the Cloisters, and had

put me, shivery and shaken, into his own bed. I saw
tears roll down his weather-beaten cheeks as he stood,
shaving, by the window; he did not seem to despise
me, a boy old enough to be already in the VIII, because
I was crying on his pillows. After that, of course, I
was Warre's man for life. Yet even at that moment
I became strangely the Headmaster's critic. For I heard
him, at his dressing-room door, dictate the telegrams
to be sent to the fathers of the two dead boys: 'Very
grave news. Come at once. Edmond Warre.' Colonel
Horne was in the North of Scotland. I, who had suffered all the agonies of bereavement during the few
seconds that elapsed between my seeing 'Wreck of
H.M.S. *Flora*' on a poster and buying a newspaper,
knew instantly that the wording of those telegrams was
cruelly wrong. The truth can never be so devastating
as suspense; I knew that Colonel Horne should have
been told that his boy had died, and in what circumstances, and was haunted all that day by the thought of
Colonel Horne's journey southward, and of that point
in his journey that would bring him face to face with a
poster, an evening paper and the heart-rending truth.
For the little boy had died because his windows were
barred: the whole House had been helpless in the road
watching a white face at the bars, while my tutor, R. S.
Kindersley, had made gallant but hopeless attempts at
the top of a ladder to prise the bars open with a crow-
bar. Flames and intolerable heat had beaten him back,
singed and blackened and despairing. This was the
story that Colonel Horne would read, at latest when
he reached London. I suppose I should have suggested
to Warre that his telegrams would not do; and had I
done so, I believe now that he would have listened to

me, for he was essentially humble. But I had not, at the time, the courage to speak.

I do not think that Kindersley ever got over the fire. A few weeks before that first of June when a quiet, rather uninteresting boy, already a member of the Upper Boats, got out of bed at about four o'clock and made a bonfire of kindling wood in a cupboard beneath the single wooden staircase, several of the Lower boys had pointed out to m'tutor the danger they would be in from their barred windows in the case of fire. M'tutor agreed; but structural alterations had to have the consent of the Bursar; he would speak to the Bursar about it. It slipped his memory, until the moment when he saw Horne at the window. Can it ever have escaped his memory again? Another boy, Noel Bligh, could not sleep that night. He felt worried about the bars, so got out of bed and worked on them with a file until they were thin enough to snap by hand. He then went to bed and to sleep; at four o'clock he woke, like the rest of us, to find the house in flames. Like the rest of us, he opened his door; the passage was gone, the stairs were gone, the interior of the house was a red-hot furnace. Like the rest of us, he closed his door and went to his window, broke the filed bars, and climbed down into the street by means of the enormous wistaria which spread its tough and life-saving ropes all over the ancient wooden south face of my tutor's.

It is curious that none of the forty boys, all in pyjamas and slippers, who scrambled down the wistaria, or let themselves drop into the churchyard on the north side of the house, noticed at the time that M. was fully dressed, in shoes, trousers, blazer, and cap. We did know that he had been the first to run through Eton

shouting 'fire', but that he was then fully dressed was
not noticed. Three nights later, a Lower boy named
Levett, at Mr. Rawlins' house, heard, in the middle of
the night, steps in the passage. He peeped out, and saw
M., who had been temporarily taken in at Rawlins',
carrying paper and firewood. Levett followed him.
He saw the bigger boy go to the foot of the main staircase, make a heap of wood and paper, and set it alight.
Levett went back to his room, fetched a water-jug, and
put the small bonfire out. He then took a chair, and
spent the rest of the night sitting on guard outside M.'s
room, into which he had seen M. return. Levett, a
Fourth Form boy, did not choose to disturb his tutor
or the House when he himself was capable of handling
the situation.

The first reaction of us all to this story was that the
fire, which gave to many of us recurrent nightmares,
had caused M. to walk in his sleep. But once attention
was focused on this boy, it was soon established that he
had been seen in the streets, already far from the house
and fully dressed, at the very moment that the rest of
us were sliding down the wistaria. There were rumours
that he had confessed. The authorities were secretive,
but M. disappeared.

R. S. Kindersley, whose life was broken in halves
by this tragedy, became my house-tutor when Lowry
went to Tonbridge as Headmaster in 1900. I have been
told that when Barrie's *Admirable Crichton* first appeared
in London, a poll of the Eton Masters was held, to
decide which of them, in the unlikely case of the whole
staff being cast away together upon a desert island,
would rise to the position of Crichton. Names had to
be given in order of preference. The lists handed in

were unanimous in respect of two names only. All put Kindersley first; all put Arthur Christopher Benson last.

We should have agreed with the Masters about m'tutor's fitness to lead us on a desert island. A man of splendid masculine looks, an outstanding oar and player of Rugby football, hardy, ascetic, and practical, he was a great sailer of boats, an accomplished carpenter and 'handyman'. We genuinely admired him; we all came, in time, to be fond of him. But until the time of the fire (after which the sight of a man broken in spirit and only by immense efforts able to return to his work and play moved to compassion even our schoolboy hearts) we were always at loggerheads with him. He was completely lacking in imagination. He had no sympathy whatever with the customs and traditions of Eton. He tried to deprive us of a House Library, 'a room for idling'. He never said 'Of course I take your word for it' without insisting on proofs and corroborations. He had never felt cold in his life, and so we froze in the Winter Halves. He had never noticed what he ate; so our food, though sufficient, was dishearteningly monotonous. There is no doubt but that boys bored him stiff; he had no conversation for us at the Boys' Dinner where he carved, silent and depressed. Practice wall-games were played 'after twelve'. I played 'wall' and was exhausted by the long bullies, and could not eat at dinner. M'tutor called me to his study. 'I'm sorry to see, Jones, that you "sock" in the mornings; it's a bad example to the younger boys.' ('Socking' meant eating sweet stuff between meals.) I had been Captain of his House for four years when I received this rebuke; I was Captain of the Boats, a

member of the VIth Form, and in the strictest possible
training for St. Andrew's Day and the House Ties. So
little did Kindersley know about boys. His rather
heroic life was a tragedy of miscasting. I call it heroic
because he knew full well that he had capacities which
he could not exercise, and had been allotted a part he
could not play. He was dutiful, loyal, and unflinching,
and in all our petty quarrels with him we never lost our
sense of his strength and fineness. His tragedy was
never to be cast away upon a desert island.

The Grand Old Man among the Masters was Henry
Luxmoore. Austere, ascetic, and, except towards the
boys in his own House, aloof, Luxmoore stood next to
Warre in capacity for inspiring awe. His stern old face,
framed in rather long grey locks, was severely handsome. He was of the eagle type, with an eye that
quelled you; grim-mouthed, lined, and a little weary.
How had Luxmoore come by those deep furrows, that
high look of severity not untouched by suffering?
What inward conflicts, what tremendous conquests over
what spiritual enemies, had given to this man of a quiet
and easy life a mask so grim and yet so noble? He had
been all his life a schoolmaster; he had leisure and books
and a garden, and his dear Chapel services; he lived in
the place he loved best; he had faith and piety. And
he looked as if he had borne the responsibility of
Empires, and had fought, not unscarred, with devils.

My father had been 'up to' Luxmoore, and I was
up to Him more than one half. Memories of Luxmoore
in division will always be mixed up with his most individual voice. It was deep, and extraordinarily 'rich';
in a fat man it might almost have been called fruity;
but Luxmoore was slight and lean, and the sonorous,

vibrant tones that issued from his sinewy throat were rather surprising. Irony was his ferule: 'Don't talk, Phillips; remember you are not in Chap-pell.' His favourite vein was to pretend that we, so many of us from country homes, knew nothing of husbandry. I rather think I first got into his good books by interrupting one of these tirades in school: 'But I *have* driven a plough, sir; I *do* know young wheat from barley, and I know what a shingled roof is, too, Sir!' My early life as a farmer stood me in good stead, just as our browsings in the Cranmer Library had enabled us to score, in Lower Remove, over the matter of Ruskin. At any rate, Luxmoore used to ask me to tea on Sundays, where I heard young Gerald Wellesley (now Duke of Wellington) describe Murillo's paintings as 'several lumps of sugar melted in a saucer of very rich cream'. Murillo was only a name to me then; and I was revolted at hearing Wellesley, a boy who had no colours, snub the great man, who had been telling us what a grand painter Murillo was. Luxmoore's delighted chuckle, and the ensuing discussion when he talked to Wellesley as to a fellow connoisseur, put me a good deal out of countenance. I had hoped to hear Wellesley rent to pieces for his confounded cheek.

I rather think Luxmoore felt himself to be, at Eton, a lone standard-bearer for aesthetics. And indeed we got little enough guidance from anybody else. Archibald Thorburn stood to me for painting, with his pictures of grouse coming over the guns, or of a snipe on her nest. Luxmoore's taste was largely inspired by piety and morals; he ranked Watts' 'Sir Galahad', which hung in Upper Chapel, more highly than I, in maturity, have been able to rank it; but he did, at these

Sunday teas, open our Philistine eyes, and lead us to
some green pastures still unexplored by us, including
his own famed garden across the humped bridge. I
should love to know what Luxmoore, most loyal of
men, thought in his heart of his colleagues, of C. M.
Wells, Grecian and cricketer and lover of wines and
food, of 'Mike' Mitchell, the eternal schoolboy, and
even of Warre himself, whose broad scholarship and
humanity embraced, so far as we boys ever discovered,
no feeling for art. But I should love, still more dearly,
to know how Luxmoore got his iron face.

Henry Broadbent, to whom I was up for three
Halves, was another 'character' whom I cannot by any
means imagine as a contemporary of my own. Ponderous, rolling, Johnsonian, with shaggy moustache and
eyebrows, he croaked and grunted at his division, curt
and epigrammatic, as if it was more than he could bear
to have to do with us three times a day. And yet there
was a large patience about him; he liked the boy who
hesitated over his construe if the hesitation was to find
the right, not the easy, equivalent; he always assumed
that we were trying; and we guessed at, and trusted in,
his native benevolence. 'Keep your eyes pure, Wodehouse', was a surprising growl, till we tumbled to it
that Wodehouse, bred like myself among Norfolk
labourers, was inclined, like them, to say 'loike'. Mr.
Broadbent, for all his huge bulk, played a good game of
fives, and could be seen, any March afternoon, steaming and stamping, like Eliot's cab-horse, in the court
marked 'H.B.' And on a summer evening he liked to
double-scull, with a competent wet-bob at bow, a boat-
load of boys downstream to the Bells of Ouseley, where
an enormous tea, with buttered eggs and scones, awaited

us in the private room, exhaling the scent of beer and furniture polish.

'Broader' had pluck. One summer evening he was potting plants, bending over the pots and displaying a vast, tight area of bottom. From a window of Tatham's gaunt house that overlooked Broadbent's garden, a boy with a catapult took careful aim and scored a bull's-eye with a stinging pellet. The bulky man could not turn quickly; by the time he had heaved himself round, every window in Tatham's house was blank. He was resolved what to do. He called Mrs. Broadbent: 'Alice, kindly conceal yourself behind that curtain and watch the windows opposite.' Mrs. Broadbent obeyed. Broadbent again bent over his pots,

> Atqui sciebat quae sibi barbarus
> Tortor pararet,

and, sure enough, he received another stinging shot in the rump. But Alice had spotted the assassin, and justice was done.

Broadbent was reputed to read the whole of *The Times* between breakfast and Chapel. Mr. Conybeare decided to test him. He discovered a short paragraph in small print recording that John Smith had been fined for stealing a pair of green-and-yellow check trousers. At Chambers he threw the question across the room. 'What were the bags, Broader?' 'Er — green and yellow check.'

I had a particular friend at Broadbent's whom we called Percy. There was a standing joke, of some obscure origin which I have forgotten, that Percy should be greeted at the beginning of each Half with: ''Ullo, Percy, 'ow's farver?' Percy had to reply 'Doing a bit, doing a bit,' and go through the motions of a

man on a treadmill. At the beginning of one Half we
found ourselves in a tight corner: we could neither
greet Percy with the usual question, nor look him in
the face while we omitted it. For during the holidays
Percy's father had been sent to prison for a bucket-shop
swindle, with the maximum publicity, and was in very
truth doing a bit. I learned, later on, that this non-
conforming parent had for many halves neglected to
pay any school fees. Mr. Broadbent had paid for
Percy out of his own pocket. No wonder his House
swore by this ungainly, gruff, learned, and good-hearted
man.

Mr. Rawlins, who took Division II, was a character
who seemed, on first acquaintance, to have no character, professionally speaking. He did not seem aware
of being a schoolmaster or of ourselves as schoolboys.
Urbane, polite, and formal, carefully dressed and well
brushed, he was a man of the world who, it seemed,
had been asked to oblige by discoursing to some younger
men of the world upon the *Annals* of Tacitus. He
assumed that we came into school of our own accord,
out of curiosity about some interesting Romans of
importance, and that we were gentlemanly, considerate,
punctual, and studious young people. And when up
to this seemingly rather colourless man, we did in fact
become punctual, studious, and considerate. What is
more, we found his Romans to be very much alive,
and our curiosity about the misunderstood Tiberius
and 'the horrible Julia' was in fact aroused. We might
have been young men at Brooks', listening to some
senior member's memories of Gladstone and Mrs.
O'Shea. On the first and last days of the Half, he
formally shook hands with us all.

N

'Toddy' Vaughan was tiny, really tiny, with next to no neck. He was lion-hearted, humble, dignified, unself-conscious, and ardent. He would ride horses too hot for his small strength. On field-days Quartermaster Vaughan was frequently bolted with, generally into the enemy's lines. He had a wall-eye, and a perpetual sniff. He was the perfect 'butt' for schoolboys. And there was not a better loved or more respected Master, which says almost as much, I think, for the boys as for this gallant little man. Vaughan ran the Shakespeare Society for older boys who cared to join. We met in his private drawing-room at night, drank coffee, ate delicious little sandwiches, and read the Plays, having been allotted our parts by Vaughan, who himself took all the murderers and messengers. Selwyn K.S., the present Dean of Winchester, Captain of the School, Newcastle scholar, a distinguished player of the Field Game, and a popular 'Pop', was a leading light at these gatherings. But they were not an unalloyed pleasure to him. Shakespeare sometimes uses words at which the pure-minded must blush. Gordon was pure-minded, but had somehow managed to acquire these words, and he always blushed. He did not, however, himself pronounce them. If they occurred in his own part he skipped them. On one occasion Gordon paused in full career. He did not, for once, know the word, but it looked fishy to him. He grew pink. He gathered himself together for the leap over its head. Toddy Vaughan was impatient. He sniffed and rubbed his nose. 'Get on, get on, Selwyn — it only means a helmet!'

Toddy once entertained some of us at dinner. Toby Albright, a member of Vaughan's own house, and a

renowned mimic, ventured, after unaccustomed claret
and port, to give the conventional imitations of the
leading 'beaks'. Toddy was delighted. 'Very good,
very good, Albright. And now, how do you do me?'
'Oh, we don't do you, Sir.'
'Nonsense! Of course you do me. Let us have it.'
'Well, Sir, if you insist—'
'I do insist.'

Albright sniffed, rubbed his fingers into his snuffling
nose, and held them out to be shaken: 'How do you,
how do you do!' Toddy reflected a moment. He
then sniffed, rubbed his nose, and extended his hand.
'Why, yes, I suppose I do. I must try to cure it.' No
wonder he helped to civilise us all.

There were notable characters among the Masters
with whom I never had the good fortune to make contacts. Prominent among them was Arthur Christopher
Benson, last in the Admirable Crichton race, but at one
time a favourite for the succession to Warre as Headmaster. This big, untidy, benign man, minor poet and
essayist, was renowned for his story-telling. Instead of
'Sunday Private', that dreary Sunday morning hour
when Lowry used to puzzle his Lower boys with Early
Fathers, Origens, and Polycarps, but never explained,
at any rate to Jones minor, how early or whose fathers,
Benson, it was said, enthralled his House with *The Luck
of the Vails*. This was long before the days when,
sitting at his College window at Magdalene, he was
killed dead by the straightest and most lethal arrow ever
aimed by the gentle 'Max'. He, too, must have been a
civiliser; his House loved him, and I should like to
have been up to him in that Division Room which
had carved over the door: 'Somebody must be last, but

nobody need be.' All the same, I must have met him
casually — was it at one of those rare dinner-parties to
which senior boys were sometimes invited?—for I still
remember the slow, sighing speech in which he told us
of his pasty-faced friend who refused to open his window at nights. Moths came in, explained the friend,
and cockroaches and things; he could not abide insects
in his room. 'But not in London,' said Benson : 'you
are going to London for six weeks; open your window
there, it will become a habit, and you will lose your
pasty face.' The friend agreed, he went to London and
opened his window, and 'he hadn't been in bed an
hour (a big sigh) before in flew (sigh) an enormous
puffin'. Useless to explain that escapes from the Zoo
are very, very rare; the friend never opened his window
again.

Then there was Mr. Booker, who had struck a match
on M. Hua's bald head, insulting both M. Hua and
France. There was a complete breach for weeks; then
friends got both parties to agree to a reconciliation; a
meeting took place and Mr. Booker publicly kissed
M. Hua on both cheeks. France was still more deeply
affronted, and a further and more prolonged estrange-
ment was the only result of the apology. But if M. Hua
was touchy on points of honour, he was a rare bird
among French masters. Without severity or sternness,
he had complete control of his Division. Worldly,
witty, French in appearance to the point of caricature,
he kept order by sheer force of personality. At nights,
in his own cosy sitting-room, he took a small class of
candidates for the Prince Consort's Prize, and there we
learnt, not only the set books, but to gossip in French.
M. Hua spent his winter holiday at Monte Carlo; he

allowed himself a fixed sum with which to gamble;
when it was lost, he came home; if he won, he went
on playing until it was lost. He dined frequently with
King Edward VII; he stayed at the Castle to coach the
young Princes — 'Ah, my boy, champagne every night
and golf wid de 'askell ball!' He loved life and pleasure
and jokes; he made no attempt to improve or to
strengthen our moral fibres; but he also loved French
literature and was without cynicism, and was as much
a favourite, I believe, with Dr. Warre as with our new
zestful Monarch. We, his pupils, delighted in him, and
I am sure he was good for us. As an Ambassador of
France to British schoolboys, he was invaluable. Who
would not be disposed to like and admire the countrymen of this bald, black-bearded, twinkling little
man?

I was fortunate to be one of those who sat in M.
Hua's parlour, but it was M. Cuvelier, deplorable-look-
ing and most defenceless of men against 'ragging' in
Division, who taught me that there is no tonic accent
in French (which explains why French poetry sounds
so much better read by an Englishman than by a
Frenchman) and that the final é in 'été' must rhyme
with the 'y' in 'city'. And it was M. Cuvelier who
coached me for 'Speeches', so successfully that after
my playing of Dr. Pancrace on the Fourth of June, I
was told that Lord Curzon, who had aggrandized the
audience, wished me to be presented to him. I went
up blushing and fully expecting compliments, but I got
none. 'I want to shake hands with you because I myself played Dr. Pancrace thirty years ago, and was much
commended for my performance.' I hope I looked
more interested than I felt, for on this occasion my own

performance had seemed to me to be the one to be
talked about.

But my best of good fortunes was to be a History
Specialist under Mr. C. H. K. Marten, afterwards, as
Sir Henry Marten, a much-loved Provost. 'Shee-Kay'
was a born teacher. His famous 'Syllabuses', in brown
paper covers, which 'potted' the Half's period for our
young minds, substituted for the usual dates and facts
what people of the period had said about each other or
about the events of the day — 'Little Sidney Godol-
phin, never in the way and never out of the way,' 'How
much the greatest and how much the best!' — they
stayed with me for years, although now, alas, faded
beyond recall. He made history contemporary. The
specialists met, not in a classroom, but in Marten's
study in Weston's Yard, where his Irish terrier, 'Shandy',
lay stretched before the fire. 'Coming in late: wude
to my dog' — these were the only offences that ruffled
his incomparable good temper. We sat on armchairs,
or upon the sofa, and criticised each other's essays
before Marten gave his verdict. Manner was as closely
scrutinised as matter; there must be no clichés, and no
fine writing either. I owe it entirely to Marten that,
with the minimum of reading or knowledge, I got a
Brackenbury Exhibition at Balliol, and very largely to
him that, destined by family tradition for Trinity,
Cambridge, I was able to persuade my father to send
me to Balliol instead. And what that has meant to me
only Balliol men will ever guess.

Marten's understudy was a very young Master,
'Tuppy' Headlam, who had been a boy at Eton in my
own time. His manners and his heart were at absurd
loggerheads. Outwardly he affected boredom and a

weary cynicism. Nobody has ever greeted old friends
more coldly, or with a more jaundiced eye. I have
seen him yawn in the face of a boy's mother while
talking to her. He complained, he denigrated, and he
was frequently sick, poor man, between schools. Inwardly he loved beauty and all fine things; he was a
wit and a staunch friend, warm-hearted and human.
When he came to have a House of his own, I was once
his guest for the night. He asked if I would care to go
round with him on the House-master's traditional 'good
night' rounds, when each room was visited in turn.
Accustomed to Lowry's and Kindersley's insipid routine
visits, I was astounded at the genius with which 'Tuppy'
suited his brief talks to each individual boy. It was a
flawless exhibition of insight, sympathy, and humour.
And yet even he had been a trifle disconcerted that day
when a distinguished General of the Brigade of Guards
had reviewed the Corps and adjudged the drill com-
petition between House Sections for a cup. Tuppy's
House Section wore horn-rimmed spectacles to a man,
as much to the surprise of their tutor as of the General,
and when numbering off had shouted, looking straight
to their front, ' — nine, ten, knave, queen, king '. They
had been favourites for the cup; they did not win it.
Tuppy himself had served in the Guards during the war,
and was able to enter into the General's feelings, but I
think he felt that, if some section had to parade in horn-
rimmed spectacles, he was glad that it had been his own.

Another young Master with whom I sat, *tête à tête*,
in his rooms in the High Street once a week my last
Summer Half was Mr. Geoffrey Winthrop Young. I
had to write essays for him on general subjects; it is
interesting to me to remember, having regard to his

own flashing and jewelled sentences, that he made me cut and prune, and throw out the epithets. But if G. W. Y.'s brilliant writing is closely examined, it will be seen that he, too, had studied and mastered the articulations of the skeleton before he clothed it with fair flesh and fine raiment. If only I had held the key that could have unlocked, on occasions, the casket of that ardent and distinguished mind! But I never did. With Renaissance good looks, reserved, and patently dwelling in a different world from that of the ordinary run of the younger 'beaks', he did not even let out to me that he was already, in those years, a giant among mountaineers and the maker of many a famous first ascent. I never remember him speaking of himself, or saying a word irrelevant to the matter in hand. He was grave and courteous and impersonal. It is clear that mine was not the sort of surface upon which he could strike a match. His report was laconic: 'This boy will write'. He could not have foreseen that Investment Bankers only draft Prospectuses. But I like to think, when I read and re-read, with unquenchable and ever renewed delight, *On High Hills* or *Mountains with a Difference*, that my lost opportunity of fifty years ago has been to some extent made up for by an autumnal friendship, coming, to me at any rate, as warm and grateful as St. Martin's summer.

Contemporaries of mine at Eton would, no doubt, have much to say of C. M. Wells, of P. V. Broke, of H. W. Tatham, of S. G. Lubbock, and of many other men of character and personality. But, except for Mr. Wells, I had no first-hand acquaintance with these men, each of whom, for many boys through many years, stood close to the centre of Eton's small but crowded

stage. And 'Bummy' Wells, who tried to teach me
Greek composition in Division I, had, for me, besides
his sad addiction to stamp collecting, another small
defect in his rich and many-sided nature. He could not
do with wet-bobs. He saw them with difficulty even
when standing up before him; he spoke to them fur-
tively out of the corner of his mouth; he liked to
pretend that they had only bodies, and no souls. Only
once did he look me in the face. I had rendered
Tennyson's 'rippled ringlets' in 'Godiva' as 'gelasmata
trichon — the laughter of her locks'. 'I might have
sent you up for that, Jones,' he murmured. I'm afraid
he meant, 'if your pluperfect hadn't had been so im-
perfect', but I suspected him, at the time, of meaning
'if you hadn't been an oaf of a wet-bob '. I lost, by
my addiction to rowing, the chance of getting to know
one of the most fascinating Masters of my day.

To R. S. de Havilland, on the contrary, wet-bobs
were, as he was fond of saying, 'the salt of the earth '.
'Havvy' was the famous coach of the Eton VIII, with
a never-to-be-surpassed number of Henley victories to
his credit; it was my luck to row for three years in the
VIII and on the last occasion, as 'Skipper', to win the
Ladies' Plate. A natural hero-worshipper, I fell completely under the spell of this wizard's charms. There
was no 'master and boy' relationship between us. He
was my friend and my father-confessor, a man to whom
one could talk without reserve; a great gentleman,
eager and sympathetic, full of heart, sensible of our
sensibilities, pithy, bracing, and amused. His very
faults were endearing. Everlastingly harassed by the
most terrifying fits of coughing I have ever seen, he
could be fiercely impatient and abusive; but the ensuing

smile was like evening sunshine after storm. From the
tow-path, his denunciations were searing. In my last
year, when I rowed as Captain, he cursed me as never
before, desperately trying, I think, to make a silk purse
out of a sow's ear; but when the practice was over,
and Coach and Captain met to discuss results and plan
for the next move, he treated me as if I had been an
authority equal to himself. I cannot doubt that his
success as a coach was as much due to his freehold in
the affections of his crews as to his uncanny knowledge of the secret of boat-propulsion. Our belief and
trust in him was absolute: we loved everything about
him : his sunburnt, Spanish face, with strong hooked
nose and raven's-wing moustache; his expressive eyes,
now furious, now glinting with fun; his battered straw
hat with the faded Oxford ribbon; our own pride when
Lord Rosebery shouted 'Hullo, Havvy!' from the top
of Windsor Bridge. His rough-haired terrier, 'Legs-
you-fool', was our mascot.

Havvy failed to make a first-class oar of me, but he
taught me many values, not least the comfort and
exhilaration of possessing admirations and affections.
Incidentally, it was Havvy who, with the old town of
Henley as quarry, first opened my eyes to the compel-
ling charm of Georgian architecture. He knew how to
transmit his private enthusiasms and directed my un-
informed attention, with a strict economy of words, to
the means by which a perfect building had achieved its
perfection. If it were only for this one life-long pleasure, I should owe him much. I doubt whether Havvy
was, professionally speaking, a wholly successful Schoolmaster. He taught Army Class, and I know nothing
of his success as a teacher; rumours of his appalling

coughing-fits and occasional rages came from his schoolroom. As a House-master I had some experience of him, having boarded out with him for some weeks after Kindersley's house was burnt down. He spoilt us with salmon and strawberries for supper, and his laxity, as far as School rules went, was considerable. After a private dinner-party one summer night, we sat together on the Wall. His house, at the corner of Keate's Lane, loomed up dark before us. From a boy's room high up, an arm was extended over the street, and the ash flicked off from the end of a glowing cigar. Smoking was a 'swishing' offence. Havvy nudged me with his elbow: 'Did you see that? The rascals!' And we continued to chat together beneath the summer stars.

Discipline is as necessary in a school as in an army, and tolerance, great virtue as it is, can be misplaced. But one can't have everything, and, on balance, I am sure that it did us far more good to be the devoted 'fans' of a man of Havvy's rare quality than it did us harm to be over-indulged. For me, at any rate, Havvy contributed more than any Master of my time to the romance, the responsibility, and the enlargement of growing up. Diverse as they were, I think it can be fairly said that our Masters had one thing in common: unworldliness. Their own variegated values had nothing to do with money or social, as apart from professional, success. If Luxmoore was ascetic and Wells a lover of good wine, both valued scholarship for its own sake, not for its prizes. And, with the exception of R. H. Mitchell, I do not think there was a single 'beak' who did not try, at all events, to dilute with one or other of the humanities the strong spirit of athleticism which we boys, all too willingly, swallowed.

For there is no doubt that, for most of us, to excel at some game was the main preoccupation of our lives. My own ambition was unbounded. To collect colours; to multiply the number of caps hanging from the corners of my pictures; to be able to ring the changes in the matter of scarves and stockings: no Colonel Bramble longed for brevets and decorations more ardently than I for these outward tokens of achievement. I knew, of course, as well as the next boy how to hide my feelings, and how to wear each fresh scarf with becoming modesty and insouciance. But inwardly I sucked success as a child sucks a sweet. And when, in my last year, I had ten caps to choose from, I liked to linger over the choice. Balliol, of course, cured me of all such foolishness. But I have never regretted it, for those coloured caps worked something out of my system early, and for good. I have never again felt the faintest interest in honours and rewards, and have been able, thanks to a boyish experience, to see my contemporaries win the distinctions they have so well deserved with pleasure unspotted by envy. I had my fun at School, and there has been nothing but satisfaction in seeing others have their fun later in life.

None the less, I am on the side of the Masters who tried to play down our obsession with games. Etonians in my day were led, influenced, and often dazzled by the twenty-six members of 'Pop', and except for the Captains of the School and of the Oppidans, it was rare for any boy to be elected to the Eton Society unless he was pre-eminent at one game or another. Resplendent in stick-up collars, coloured waistcoats, and buttonholes, carrying pop-canes when watching School matches, parading arm-in-arm, and allowed to carry a book in

the hand, poised for leg-slapping, instead of only under
the arm like the common herd, we 'Pops' undoubtedly
lorded it, and felt ourselves to be, as we were, a race
apart.   It would have been good for us, and for the
School, if boys of intelligence, wit and, originality,
however inept at games, had been allowed to achieve
prominence and leadership.   For many a member of
'Pop', as for myself, his best friend had to remain outside
the privileged circle.

It must be admitted that a stranger visiting Eton
would have found in the members of 'Pop', for all the
purely athletic qualifications which had landed them in
that select society, the most attractive of the boys.   But
that is because nothing improves the character like
popularity.   To be liberated from self-consciousness,
social fears and suspicions, heart-burnings and anxieties,
and to step into the sunshine of easy self-confidence,
frankness, and gaiety, does a boy a world of good.   He
can be himself;   make what was unfashionable fashionable;   bring warmth to the outcast and encouragement
to the dispirited.   Boys, like grown-up persons, are at
their best when sure of themselves, and happiness is by
no means the least of the foods upon which virtue is
nourished.   All the more reason why it would have
been well had the true élite among us become the
unofficial but recognised leaders of the School.

I believe popularity did promote virtue in us.   For
I am certain that the besetting vice of the School in
my day was social unkindness.   There was no physical
bullying, but there was a great deal of mental suffering
needlessly inflicted, and perhaps most of all by the sin
of inconstancy.   Nothing is more harassing to a young
spirit than to be taken up one day and dropped the

next; to be suddenly caballed against; to be cut, for
no known reason, by last Half's acquaintances in Division. It is extraordinary to me that this vice was never
preached against in Chapel; that nobody attempted to
make us see the cruelty of it all. Our preachers were
obsessed with impurity, or with our devotional obliga-
tions; I never remember hearing a word about unkindness. And it was rife. I recollect, with shame, a mon-
strous case in my own House. For about three years or
more three of us had 'messed' together contentedly.
Then, suddenly, at the beginning of one Half, two of
us decided to drop the third member of the mess. We
two were getting on, I suppose, socially and at games;
he, a delightful, cheerful, unselfish little boy, was still
obscure. We decided that he was a bore, and, uglier
still, discovered him to be a Jew. We not only kicked
him out of the mess, but made him the butt of our
nascent wit. He never remonstrated, but he must have
suffered cruelly; and I still blush to think of our cold-
hearted dealings with a simple and affectionate boy.
He retained his own virtue; for in after life I had contact with him again, and he bore no grudge whatso-
ever, but was all friendliness. But I cannot help thinking that if our heartlessness had been brought home to
us, we should have repented. Having achieved our
own ambitions, we did, at long last, begin, through
happiness, to see the less fortunate with new eyes.

There was also the case of 'Jerry'. Jerry was bad at
books and worse at games; he had a nervous habit of
flapping his arms against his sides like a crowing cock;
his only solace in his lonely backwater was to read and
re-read the paper-covered works of Nat Gould. We
found it irresistible, in idle moments, to visit Jerry in

his dreary little room, and to sharpen our wits upon him in the most fantastic and elaborate ways. He was utterly defenceless; without a vocabulary, without the spirit to turn upon his tormentors, he could only stand and flap miserably while we flapped back at him, and invented new chapters in the endless Jerriad which bewildered him as much as it tickled us. Actually, we were fond of Jerry, and regarded him as a kind of mascot; but he can never have guessed it, and I think, with remorse, of what a little more kindness, and much less chaff, might have meant to this fish out of water. It is pleasant to remember that at Christchurch Jerry, who was a capital horseman, came into his own, and was a popular member of the Bullingdon Club. Here, again, happiness transformed him. A curious aspect of this besetting sin is that while most of us suffered from it, as well as committing it, our suffering did not amend us. I sat next to a charming and good-looking boy in Division one Half, and we became friends, taking Sunday walks together. It was an Easter Half, when the School sports are held. W. won most of the Junior events, and became known to the whole School overnight as an outstanding young athlete. He was gracious when I congratulated him, but after that never spoke to me again, although we continued to sit side by side in school and chapel. As far as I was concerned, he had died on the day of the sports, and gone to Heaven. I was deeply wounded at the time, but lived to endure a far more bitter hour when, the first time I was put up for 'Pop', I was heavily blackballed. My friend and proposer reported that two formidable 'Pops' at another house had each dropped in six black balls, amid laughter, but unseen by the President, because they disliked my

face. I had never spoken to either, and it was a shock
to discover that one's face can shatter all one's dearest
ambitions. I became aggressive, surly, and shy. The
next Half my enemies had either left the School or
switched their hostility to some other face, and I was
elected. I became friendly, sunny, and even kind. I am
convinced that compassion is not learnt by suffering,
but is the fruit of happiness; that to experience social
unkindness leads not, as one might hope, to fellow-
feeling, but to aggressiveness; and that if I was a Headmaster, I should be more concerned with the vice of
unkindness than with any other moral failing in my
School. Headmasters and House-masters are supposed
to be ridden by the nightmare of physical impurity, but
although there was, as there must be among a herd of
adolescent boys, plenty of bawdy talk, and a fashion of
imputing homosexual 'affairs', generally quite unjustly,
to prominent figures in the School, the thing itself was,
in those days, uncommon enough. And there was one
mitigating feature which, puritanical as I was in my
attitude to the vice, although not to the bawdy conversations, which afforded openings for the exercise of wit
and even humour, I discovered, somewhat to my surprise, for myself. The black sheep of the School were
almost invariably boys of kind hearts and frank, open
natures. One particular black sheep, himself a great
athlete, was, I think, the nicest boy I knew in his relations with the obscure and the unsuccessful. He had a
good word for and to everybody. And it must never be
forgotten that, in a school, homosexuality is a mere sub-
stitute for heterosexuality. It would not exist if, as we
are told is the case in Canada and the U.S.A., girls were
accessible. It was not carried beyond the leaving-day.

An Archbishops' Commission has, since the Second
World War, 'deplored' the Englishman's habit of
identifying religion with ethics. At Eton, in the early
nineteen hundreds, even our pastors and masters were
guilty of this heresy. Although, as has been said, no
two men or boys can have the same picture of 'God' in
their minds, and accordingly over a thousand Gods were
daily worshipped in Upper and Lower Chapels, we were
supplied with a common stock of notions from which
to construct, each for himself, our idea of Godhead. It
was common ground, for Dr. Warre as much as for
Jones minor, that an essentially male God, Omnipotent
and Omniscient, had created the Universe; that, after
untold billions of years, He had decided to people an
insignificant planet in a lesser galaxy with a race of
potentially immortal spirits; that He had created these
spirits stained with Original Sin, that He might, eventually, redeem them; that nearly 2,000 years ago He had
put into action His plan of salvation by sending to earth
His Son, Who by His death and Resurrection atoned
for man's guilt and conquered both Sin and Death; and
that, since that date, those who had the good fortune to
be born in such parts of this planet as made it practicable
for them to be baptized, taught the Faith and confirmed
in it, would be redeemed from sin and enjoy, after death,
Everlasting Life. (What happened to the millions of
human beings who lived before the Coming of His
Son, or to those who, after that event, had no chance of
hearing about it, was never explained.) To the above
notions was added the very important ones that God
was a God of Love, Mercy, and Forgiveness, and that
He was, above all, anxious for us to be Good. We
were never, I am certain, afraid of God. And we

o

believed that He heard our prayers, even if He seemed
slow to answer them.   I cannot remember now whether
it was in Upper Chapel that I first developed misgivings
as to the potency of formal supplications, carefully
intoned by a Conduct chosen for his correct ear and
melodious voice.   I probably assumed that for all the
lack of genuine, heartfelt pleading behind them, they
were somehow — perhaps for their beauty? — ex-
empted from the condemnation given by Jesus to 'vain
repetitions'.   In the same way I have little doubt that,
because I liked the tunes and enjoyed singing, I had no
sense of the inept anthropomorphism by which love of
hearing Himself praised was attributed to a Supreme
Being.   It is staggering, on reflection, to remember the
near-blasphemies, upon any spiritual conception of a
Deity, which we all, clergy, masters, and boys alike,
took for granted.

I can recollect no teaching which would have enabled
us to see Jesus as the hero that He was, the moral genius
and revolutionary whose 'inner light' convinced Him
that the human psyche is kin to a cosmic and imperish-
able Spirit, willing goodness.   Nobody pointed out to
us the momentous implications of such a saying as 'The
Kingdom of Heaven is within you'.   No steps were
taken to erase from our young minds the false and, to
boys, distasteful image of a meek, epicene, long-haired
Figure, as far removed as can be from the valiant, com-
pelling prophet of the Gospels.   There can be no more
damning testimony to the failure of Christian teaching
in a public school fifty years ago than the shocking fact
that a House-master in Holy Orders could be familiarly
known as 'Creeping Christ'.   Through whose fault did
sanctimoniousness come to be associated in our minds

with the name of the bravest and most lovable of man-
kind? It is easy to blame our teachers; but it must be
remembered that they, in turn, had been nurtured in a
faith which, having deified a Prophet who forbade men
even to call him 'Good', let alone 'God', had lost sight
of his towering and vivid personality behind the un-
touchable veils of ecclesiastical 'Holiness'. And so we
were left without guidance to make what we could of
the confused images impressed upon our unreflecting
minds by the pictures in the *Child's Bible* or in stained-
glass windows; by the Gospel stories read aloud, dis-
jointedly, in clerical tones; by strange talk of the
conquest of sin, which yet was rife; by the puzzle of a
Man Who, being also God, must have prayed fervently
to Himself; by the intimidating hush-hush in which all
'sacred' things were spoken about; by hymns that sang
of fountains filled with Emmanuel's blood; and, later,
by our own fitful speculation as to the fate of the untold
millions born too early, or too far off, to share in the
Redemption. Is it surprising that on weekdays we put
the whole complicated business out of our heads, as
irrelevant to our own affairs, acquiescing, on Sundays,
without criticism and without interest, in whatever
Authority provided for us? But Authority cannot
easily be forgiven for permitting our confusion, or our
indifference, to be such as could result in that inept and
deplorable nick-name given, I am sorry to say, to more
than one of our Pastors.

What instruction we had in the Scriptures was given
through 'Sunday Questions'. These were set by our
Division Master, and had to be answered in our own
time on Sundays, so inevitably linking in our minds
the Bible with a distasteful task. Until, in the higher

Divisions, we had to wrestle with St. Paul's epistles and the commentators, 'Sunday Qs' for the most part took us at large through the Old Testament. 'Yahveh' having been unluckily translated as 'the Lord', an expression accepted by our teachers as by ourselves as representing the very God whom we worshipped in Chapel, we learnt, Half by Half, how this 'great and terrible God' had threatened to 'execute vengeance in anger and fury upon the nations'; had ordered His people 'to slay both man and woman, infant and suckling, ox and sheep, camel and ass'; had slain Uzzah for putting out a hand to steady the Ark; had killed 70,000 innocent men and women because David took a census, and had commanded the inhabitants of Palestine to be utterly destroyed; how His 'day' was to come, 'cruel both with wrath and fierce anger, to lay the land desolate'; how He 'smote with blasting and with mildew and with hail' because His temple was not rebuilt; how He burnt up Nadab and Abihu for 'offering strange fire', and had refused offerings from a flat-nosed man; how He ordered the perpetual slavery of foreigners, and, but for the intercession of Moses, would have destroyed His own people for being down-hearted at the defeatist report of the spies; how He had commanded a man to be stoned to death for gathering sticks on the Sabbath, and had destroyed Korah, Dathan, and Abiram 'with all their little ones', burnt 250 of their followers, and slain 14,700 people on the following day for blaming Moses for this cruelty; how He approved the wholesale massacres of Joshua, and struck Uzziah with leprosy for usurping a priestly function. These are but a few samples of the goings-on of this fierce tribal God whom we were expected to equate with a God of Love. Moreover, it

was the men of action in the Old Testament whose
lives were our particular study, these favourites of 'the
Lord' whose careers were even, by some priestly kink,
supposed to 'typify' or 'foreshadow' the life of Jesus
Himself. Jacob, who would today be called a 'crook';
Joshua and David, who both committed the most horrid
atrocities on innocent people in war; Elijah, who burnt
up two separate companies of 50 innocent soldiers for
obeying superior orders; Elisha, who had 42 children
torn by bears. For some reason our attention was less
often drawn to the prophets and poets, to Amos, Hosea,
Isaiah, and Micah, who turned against the contemporary conceptions of a war-like and cruel Deity, and
attributed to the God of their people loving-kindness
and mercy and righteousness and wisdom. Were our
Form-masters perhaps not altogether unwilling that we
should draw our own conclusions from our studies?
And may the steady decline in church-going since those
days be due, in part, to the failure of the Churches,
before it was too late, to recognise those ancient writ-
ings for what they are, and to distinguish, once and for
all, a God who can be nothing if not Good from the
ogreish Yahveh?

We got little guidance from the Sunday morning
and evening sermons. The Home Team of preachers,
although diverse, were prophets in their own country,
and did not have our full attention. The provost, Dr.
Hornby, elegant figure-skater and after-dinner speaker,
was wholly inaudible. The Rev. S. A. Donaldson, a
good-hearted and popular House-master (who had once
coached the VIII), had a tenor voice, celebrated for its
brio in 'Onaway! awake, Beloved!' at the School Concerts. It hit the Chapel roof with ease in its opening

phrase: 'Isn't it a *terrible* thought, that we are here in the
house of *God*?'—delivered in an impassioned crescendo.
Down the rows of sleek Sunday heads, of abstracted
young faces, there was no responsive quiver. If the
thought was still terrible to the preacher, he had made
it so familiar to his hearers as to rob it of its terrors.
One Sunday the preacher discovered another cause for
trembling. Watching a House-match, he had heard
a young player say 'Damn you'. 'Isn't it a *terrible*
thought, that a boy should call upon His Maker to
condemn a playmate to everlasting punishment?' This
thought also was received with stoic fortitude by the
congregation.

The Rev. T. C. Porter, the Science Master, can
hardly be counted. He preached once in Lower Chapel,
but was so amusing that he never preached again.

Visiting preachers in Upper Chapel, when too courteous to impute impurity to their young hosts, had a
tendency to preach about George Augustus Selwyn,
first Bishop of New Zealand and Indonesia. Unfor-
tunately this great and good man became, through
repetition, our Aristides. And when, after an eloquent
catalogue of his virtues, during which the name had
been cunningly withheld, the preacher came to the
inevitable climax: 'Need I say, boys, that I refer to that
greatest and best of Etonians' — a low muttering of
'George Augustus Selwyn' took the words from the
preacher's mouth, and muffled and circumspect as the
murmur was, caused the Masters in Desk to look up
sharply from their private reveries.

And that reminds me of a sad, shameful episode.
There was a visiting preacher who should never have
been invited. Tiny, round, and red, with a voice like

Mr. Punch, he was too small for the pulpit. Whether he kept falling off his stool, or whether he was a natural 'bobber' like the dipper or the wagtail, I do not know; but throughout his sermon he appeared and disappeared over the rim of the pulpit with rhythmical alternation.[1] It would have been funny at a circus; in Chapel the effect was overwhelming. Yet nobody laughed; so small was he, that the point taken was, not the absurdity of his eclipses, but the gallantry of his reappearances. These began to be applauded, by a stamping of feet upon the wooden cross-bars of the desks — at first a controlled stamping by a small group, but one that gradually spread and swelled until every time he bobbed up again twelve hundred boots drummed out grateful acknowledgment. There was nothing he could do but go on; there was nothing the Masters could do but become engrossed in the details of the Chapel roof; even the Headmaster could only chew the inside of his cheek and gaze sternly into space. Unanimity and unprecedentedness are, in conjunction, momentarily invincible.

Next day came the inevitable summons to Upper School 'after twelve'. Never was Warre so quiet or so telling. He was not angry; he was heartbroken. He did not talk of irreverence or sacrilege. He simply said that he could not have believed that Eton boys would be rude to a guest, to an old friend of his own. There were no punishments, no deprivations. He showed us his heartbreak and left it at that. We went away thoroughly ashamed.

At the end of the period I am remembering a new

[1] Sir Edward de Stein asserts that his text was 'Be not afraid, it is I'.

era dawned. A youthful Master in College, tall, heavy-shouldered, with an unruly 'lick' of fair hair standing up above his forehead, leant easily upon the pulpit cushion one Sunday morning and began his sermon with a casual-sounding question: 'Have you ever seen a cat walk along a garden wall?' So began a revolution in Eton Chapel and a series of sermons which were to become celebrated in their day. The preacher was Dr. Cyril Alington.

I believe I am on firm ground in saying that School Authorities, fifty years ago, did indeed identify religion with ethics. We heard little, if anything, of the sacramental and salvationist side of Christianity; even Confirmation was regarded chiefly as an occasion for taking stock and for turning over a new leaf. How far our daily conduct was influenced and moderated by religion it is difficult to say. I rather think our code was that of a gentleman rather than of a Christian. But we did have consciences; and conscience, that lies deep, is a more potent force than any code. In any case, boys do not talk about such things; we affected, among ourselves, to be a stiff-necked and hard-hearted generation, but we were not pagans. My own case was untypical, since about two years after my brother's death my parents were given what seemed to them, and still seems to me, to be sufficient proof that we survive, complete with our memories and personalities, bodily death. This restored to my mother her faith and love of life, and happiness to my home and holidays. But it also gave me a view of human destiny, and of what may be called 'the means of grace', in which institutional religion could have no place, and least of all the theology and cosmogony of the churches. The whole orthodox 'Plan of Salvation' became, for me, nothing but 'foolishness'. I had, as I thought and think now, sufficient evidence that it was all a mistake. So that, at fifteen years old, I had my private reasons for being immune for life from credal preoccupations, conscious, perhaps to an unusual degree for my age, of the reality, behind the visible world, of another order of life and thought and activity. It is a good deal to be certain of, although it solves, of itself, none of the problems of Good and Evil, of the nature of Godhead, of freedom or determinism. But one has something to look forward to.

No doubt this private conviction of mine has coloured my recollections of the spiritual sustenance offered to us. The Dean of Winchester may well have a different story to tell. But I think I am right about the official, as well as our own, view of Confirmation. I had no notion of breaking ranks by declining to be confirmed, and thought, with the rest, that it would do me good and add to my stature. But I was 'prepared' for it by my tutor, Kindersley, a layman inclined, I rather suspect, to a kind of benevolent agnosticism. He was content to hear me repeat the Creed and the Lord's Prayer, without comment, and to read the Confirmation service with me. He spared me the intimate discussions on resistance to sexual temptation from which one at least of the clerical masters sent his Confirmation-class back to their house-libraries primed with hair-raising matter to retail.

My actual Confirmation was spoilt for me by the shallowest and most unworthy of worries, which depressed me for a fortnight beforehand and distracted me, on the day itself, from the appropriate frame of

mind.   My parents, being abroad, could not attend the
ceremony, as was customary.   This was on the whole
a relief, since their visits to Eton were always anxious
occasions for me.   My mother was always perfect, both
in dress and deportment, but I was dreadfully ashamed
of my father's appearance, and had no confidence that
he would not misbehave.   The main source of my
shame was that he always wore turned-down collars.
which nobody else's father would dream of doing
except out shooting.   It is true that Mr. Arthur Balfour
wore them, but he was Prime Minister and my father
was not.   And to aggravate the deplorable effect of the
collars, his hair was too long over his ears.   That he was
strikingly handsome atoned for nothing.   Moreover,
he talked at the top of his voice, even when we were
passing 'Pops' in the street, and he had been known to
introduce himself to boys, even boys with colours,
whose fathers he had known.   He seemed to have no
sense that parents must assume their son's rank in the
school;   he made himself alarmingly at home, and
would confess, in ringing tones, that watching cricket
bored him, when standing in Upper Club itself.

    But relief turned to dismay when I received a letter
from Aunt Mary.   This aunt, a sister of my father's,
had been known to our childhood only as a critic of
our manners and morals.   After many years in India as
some sort of lay-missionary, she had emigrated to
America, to become a Fundamentalist, searching the
prophecies in an inerrant Bible for the key to her
personal salvation.   The outcome of her studies was a
satisfactory conviction that Death would come to the
Archbishops, but not to her; and that she herself, with a
group of friends, would on a certain day go to meet

her Lord in the air. After that date she would assist
Him in ruling the rest of us for a thousand years. But
at the time of my Confirmation she had not yet seen
the light, and, being on a visit to England, she wrote to
me announcing her intention of being present at the
Confirmation ceremony in company with an American
friend, and begging me to order luncheon for three at a
suitable hostel. I would, had I dared, have 'scratched'.
Not daring to run out, I arranged for luncheon in a
small private room over Rowland's shop, whither the
distance to be walked from Chapel was short, and where
we should be safe from the eyes of other boys and their
parents. For if I could be uneasy about my father's
collars, I was in a fever of apprehension about Aunt
Mary's clothes. I had vague recollections of tightness
and drabness, of sensible boots, and of an even more
sensible umbrella. What I had not feared had been
buttons. But it was buttons that, in the event, wrecked
this solemn occasion in my young life. Buttons that
started close beneath Aunt Mary's cleft and self-con-
fident chin, and ran down in their serried hundreds to
just above the ground. What sort of garment they
fastened, or pretended to fasten, I cannot recollect. I
only know that these buttons, absurd as they were
conspicuous, spoilt my day. I had to find them a place
in Chapel. I had to escort them to Rowland's shop.
And so shallow was the soil that my Tutor had prepared
for the sowing, so tenuous my spirituality, that I had
no moral resources, on this day of days, which I was
able to mobilise and to deploy against the onslaught
of a row of buttons. They got me, as they held
me, down. It was a brilliant and successful stroke of
Satan's. I was only partially restored at luncheon by

the American friend who, on hearing that I was in the Eight, replied that her nephew had achieved a like honour at his College in Arkansas. He was, she said, in the Singing Eight. It was the measure of our Philistinism that this was treated by myself and my friends as a tremendous joke. That the art of making music should be equated with the art of propelling a boat seemed to us the height of transpontine imbecility.

Religion is such a personal matter, and a boy's receptivity to its inculcation depends so much upon early impressions and the values held in honour in his home, that it would be risky to pass judgment upon Eton's contribution to our spiritual welfare at the turn of the century. Criticism of the general education given to us is easier to make. Latin and Greek were our main subjects, and I am convinced that there was something radically wrong with methods of teaching that left me and most of my contemporaries unable to construe an inscription on a memorial tablet, let alone to read with enjoyment an Ode of Horace or a Greek epigram. It was all right for the clever collegers, the Selwyns and Macmillans, a Ronald Knox or a Patrick Shaw-Stewart. These were born scholars, with the enviable gift of seeing and apprehending whole sentences at a glance, not, as we did, single words, lonely and adrift, or rubbing shoulders with other unrelated waifs. Should not the use of cribs, so far from being a penal offence, have been made compulsory? Is it not more sensible to read Virgil knowing what he means than not knowing what he means? Swiftness is all, in reading either verse or prose; one must get on with it, marching with the prose or dancing and swinging with the verse. As the vocabulary will come with repetition, so will the syntax become familiar; above all, interest will be excited, and with interest facility. A child, by his reading in his own language, learns a vast vocabulary never used, or heard, by him in talk. He learns grammar by ear, not rules. He is not asked to 'compose' until he has read enough to carry in his head a model that he can copy. Even as Lower boys, we made weekly Latin verses, with the help of the 'Gradus', before we had ever understood or enjoyed a single line of Latin poetry. We were like botanical students who, never having seen a live primrose, should be asked to dissect a dead one. We parsed and conjugated and declined; and left Eton with only the barest notion of the content, or the living, moving form, of the two great classic literatures. Has the experiment ever been tried of beginning Latin with St. Bernard's hymns, or the monkish Latin of the *Gesta Francorum*? 'Tunc Bohemundus, bulliens ira . . .' the words run on in accustomed order; it is a good story about fighting; it is not classical Latin, but it is Latin. Children do not begin to learn English with Shakespeare and Milton. Ought not Fourth Form to read dog-Latin, or the 'lion-Latin' of the Vulgate, and the Lower Fifth to go on to Plautus, so getting into their heads that Latin was once actually spoken? And when the vocabulary and the inflexions have become familiar through sheer frequency, the frequency given by pace and mileage, let the Upper Forms tackle, with as little loss of speed as possible, the concise and architectural language of the classic authors.

We spent many hours a week learning by heart. But what we got by heart were chunks of Ovid and Horace and Virgil and Homer, most of it by rote, since the meaning was unclear to us. It was rarely that a

Form-master was unconventional enough to allow us to learn English poetry instead. At the time of life when the memory is most retentive, and young ears open to catch the lilt and music of good verse, our aptitude was misused and our memory strained in vain repetitions. For where the sense is hidden the sound will miss the beat, or, if the beat be heard, it will strike as a mere jingle. Our fancies were not tickled, nor our minds enriched.

Mathematics were, I believe, well taught, but being one of those unfortunates who cannot add, and are so intimidated by symbols that their minds shut up in self-defence, I am not qualified to speak of them.

Science, in charge of that rubicund, unbelieving parson, Dr. Porter, was good fun, for there were experiments and explosions; but it was strictly confined to chemistry, and although I can still repeat Boyle's Law and Gay Lussac's Law about gases, I have never met anybody who wished to hear me repeat them. We were taught nothing of biology, nothing of physics, and although the starry heavens looked down upon us, we never lifted our eyes to them. Drawing was a matter of Lower boys copying plaster-casts under the eye of old Sam Evans for a couple of Halves; after that we drew no more. There was no painting, no pottery-making, no carpentry, no training of eye or hand. 'Fuggy' Byrne taught us that the Germans called a slow train a 'bumble-tug' and a fast train a 'snail-tug' and that amused us; but unless you were prepared to give up Greek, the hours spent on German were too few to count. And Greek, for those destined for Oxford or Cambridge, could not be given up. French, except for those ambitious enough to sit for the Prince

Consort's Prizes, was taught us as a dead language; there was composition, but no conversation. English was not taught at all until a boy's last year, when a few essays might be written. History, thanks to Mr. C. H. K. Marten, was taught with spirit and imagination to 'specialists', and made palatable to the school at large. We read *Westward Ho!* for Holiday Task when we were young, and Scott when adolescent, with the measure of distaste that all compulsion breeds. It was open to us to enjoy, as in my own case, choral music in the Musical Society, but, except at tea with Luxmoore, we were shown and told nothing of the great painters. But for my luck in rowing in the Eight, and so going to Georgian Henley with 'de Havvy', I might have continued for years without discovering that my grandfather, for all his virtues, had been a Goth, a Vandal, and a Hun.

Contrary to common belief, most Etonians, even in those days, were destined to earn their own livings, and knew it. The old excuse no longer served, that we should need nothing but a few classical tags to use in the House of Commons; a knowledge of boys, which in England is much the same as a knowledge of men; and what is called 'character'. And had our fitness for our diverse professions depended upon the training that Eton gave us, I think the Eton curriculum and Eton's methods of teaching fifty years ago must be severely censured. But luckily for us, we did not, in those days, expect to begin our professional lives on leaving school. Parents who could afford Eton could, for the most part, afford a university, and the practical question becomes not 'Did we learn anything at Eton?' but, 'Did we learn at Eton *how* to learn?' And to this question, I

believe the answer to be yes. At any rate I have heard
the Balliol Dons declare that they found Etonians, for
all their ignorance, the most suitable clay for their
moulding, fresh, receptive, and elastic. And I say
again, that I think the Etonians of my generation were
much beholden to our masters for their unworldliness,
their lack of preoccupation with our chances of success
in life, their belief that our point of view, our values,
counted for more than our technical equipment. And
when all is said and done, the curriculum-methods of a
public school cannot have more than a very moderate
effect. Because the natural resistance of English boys
to any form of instruction whatever is, up to the age of
eighteen or thereabouts, stubborn and strong and next
to invincible. Our hearts were given over to our
games, our friends, our social grandeurs and miseries;
we worked, if we did work, for conscience' not learning's sake; the fashion was for evasion and a mild kick
for the 'sap'. Tugs were Tugs, and could do as they
pleased, but young Southwell K.S. did not tell us a
second time, outside the schoolroom door, how he
had laughed over the sausage-seller when preparing
Aristophanes. We had no intention of seeing anything
funny in Greek. I am inclined to think that, at best,
the most enlightened teaching in a public school might
lower the age of curiosity from eighteen to seventeen.
Curiosity, at long last; curiosity as to why there are
great names in literature, in history, in science, in the
arts; curiosity as to the historical proofs for dogmas
which grew in strangeness as we acquired capacities
for reflection: it came to us like a shooting-thirst,
that makes the luncheon-basket suddenly more desirable than the sport. Had our teaching been less old-

fashioned, it might have come earlier, but had our
masters possessed less of the humanities, it might not
have come at all. There was a breadth, a poise, an
adulthood in the men who ground away so conscien-
tiously at our pebbly minds, that did, in our last year or
so, make us often quite suddenly tired of being mere
schoolboys. I was to find at Oxford young men
enough from other schools who were not tired of it.
Some of them have not become tired of it to this day.

I imagine that what we felt to be breadth in those
distant days could today be thought narrow enough. I
can recollect no consciousness, in the early nineteen
hundreds, among masters or boys, of the coming social
revolution. The first crack in our solid unawareness
came with a boy, Charles Lister, who joined the Labour
Party while still at Eton. But to the rest of us Keir
Hardie in his cloth cap was a joke. We rode on the
backs of the workers with the insouciance of the man
who sat on the back of a whale, believing it to be an
island. We were taught to be sorry for the very poor,
and went in batches to visit the Eton Mission at Hackney
Wick, but it could never have entered our heads that
some of the boys we met there might well, in our
lifetime, be among Her Majesty's Ministers. But for
all this obtuseness, this assurance of a social stability
which in fact was so soon to break up, I believe we did
acquire, unconsciously, a set of values which has enabled
many of us to accept the loss of privilege with equal
minds. If we seriously over-valued prowess at games,
we set no value at all on money or social position, and
among my thousand contemporaries I can only remember two snobs. One was a Master, whose snobbery
cost him the loss of all influence or respect; the other a

P

boy, whom we laughed at. (He stuck to his guns and, becoming a Courtier, went to Heaven in this world.) The Revolution came; and in a changed society, the Etonians who sold their country homes and took to washing-up after supper are not, I believe, among the least cheerful or the most regretful.

If duty is the first obligation for men and boys in a civilised society, happiness is the condition in which duty can best be done. We had plenty of duties and sufficient discipline at Eton, and, except for a handful of misfits, most of us were happy. Looking back over the years, it is not the high-lights, the delirious moments of personal triumph, that I see most clearly, but a procession of small delights, of sun-lit activities, in which we all shared. At the time no doubt, fiercely ambitious as I was, I should have described as the happiest day of my life that on which, with Tom Somers-Smith, I won the School Pulling and was 'hoisted', tipsy with champagne, by the god-like 'Pops' up and down the street before the Wall. And as the proudest day that which, three years later, saw the Eight, under my own captaincy, win the Ladies' Plate at Henley. But though memory has not blurred them, neither has it hung these exciting pictures on the line. There a far bigger canvas hangs, crowded and mellow, with the great trees and the red-brick towers, and the high-buttressed chapel in the background.

From the first day, every Eton boy has a room to himself, which is no small thing. For sheer cosiness, there is nothing to beat cooking sausages over a coal-fire in a tiny room, with the shabby dark-red curtains drawn, and the brown tea-pot steaming on the table. And after the rigours of the mornings, we were cer-

tainly entitled to a little cosiness at tea-time. For at my
tutor's no fires might be lit in boys' rooms till four
o'clock, however hard the frost outside, and since the
wearing of great-coats was something not 'done' except
by boys who had their house-colours or Upper Boats,
we shook and shivered from early school till dinner at
two o'clock. It is often said that colds are not caught
through cold, but I shall never believe it, for we snuffled
and snivelled through the Winter Halves, much to the
annoyance of 'the Hag', the generic name for all
matrons. Miss Hale, Lowry's 'Hag', was the daughter
of a former House-master, and although kind, had
Spartan standards. She was ready with ammoniated
quinine, but deaf to our suggestions that we had colds
because we were cold. If there is anything more bleak
than to return to your room between schools on a
winter's morning, with snow on the ground, to find
door and window open, the chairs on the table and
Bird, the boys' maid, scrubbing the linoleum floor, I
have not met with it. Bigger boys could crowd round
the fire in the House Library, but the Lower boys had
none at which to dry a handkerchief. I think we did
suffer real hardship, without being hardened by it; but
it was the only suffering of any sort that we endured,
and memory, which works on the principle of the sun-
dial, calls up a dozen times the cosiness of tea-time for
once that it summons back the shivery catarrh-ridden
mornings.

It was in those small intimate rooms, with the
Thorburns and Sporting prints on the walls, that we
met on winter nights to rag and gossip and cabal and
learn the art of self-preservation. The first rule for this
last was never to 'lose your hair'. Good temper put

on like a bullet-proof waistcoat may win no marks with the Recording Angel, but one becomes in time, by playing a part, the character portrayed, as Mr. Penley, if report is true, ended his days happily as Charley's Aunt after his five-thousandth performance. Self-restraint, enforced by prudence, turned imperceptibly to natural good-humour. And if it was bitter, as you lay in bed on the night of an election to the House Library, to hear the rush of steps pass your door and the voices shouting 'gratters' to your next-door neighbour, it was all part of the lesson that to be admitted to a Club you must first become 'clubbable'. For a House Library was an exception to the general rule that athletic distinction was the key to success at Eton. In the smaller community of the House we knew each other inside-out, and like JAH, did not rejoice in any man's legs. The weakling, the spectacled, the rabbit, was as acceptable round the Library fire as the winner of the Junior Steeplechase, and to claim the best armchair and the *Tatler* in that warm circle you had only to be a good chap. And this, I think, is the real merit of the House system in a big School, and one which outweighs the disadvantages of being compelled, by enforced propinquity, to choose your intimate companions and messmates from a limited and fortuitous list. Eton birds of a feather cannot flock together for most of their school lives, unless fate and their fathers put them down for the same House.

If I could look back dispassionately, I suppose I should have to condemn the House for being the earliest object of that kind of self-regarding patriotism which is the seed of nationalism, the curse of our Age. But I cannot look back dispassionately. When I go to the

Eton and Harrow match nowadays, and see the half-
empty Mound, and am told that the boys prefer to go
home for Long Leave and to play golf or lawn tennis,
I ought, I am sure, to rejoice in their good sense. They
want to be doing, not looking on. Well, I don't
rejoice. I sigh for the days when the Mound was pied
with black top-hats and white waistcoats, and ready to
become, at any moment, a bank of fluttering blue. I
miss the yells and the counter-yells; the small boy with
a light-blue tassel dangling from his walking-stick, whose
ears alone prevent his hat from extinguishing him; the
sallow Harrovian fathers who exist, they tell me, but
in my own sinful imagination; the little Etonian sisters,
delicately guarding their light-blue ribbons from the
strawberry mess; the massed coaches, on which all the
loveliest girls wear the same shade of blue; the walled
garden, hired by the Amhersts, where only the cold
salmon wore silver and pink, and the very dowagers
looked up at a sudden distant shout. A wicket, or a
boundary? Good news or bad? Those were the days
of E. M. Dowson, when the Harrovian players wore
heavy black moustaches, and the Harrow cricket-cap,
with its perverse arrangements of stripes, was menacing
as well as ungainly. Things could go very badly indeed,
and the fight in front of the Pavilion after the match
was a real anxiety to me, for hats, if knocked off, were
kicked and trampled, and my father's never-forgotten
overdraft cramped my style. Others battled for the
School, I to defend my hat, just as others went to the
play on the Saturday night, and we to the Zoo on
Sunday afternoon.

The brand of nationalism in which we all wallowed
at Lord's in those days, and in which I, almost alone,

still indulge once a year, was of the ugly war-provoking kind, with more artificial hatred of Harrow than natural love of Eton in it.   But the hatred was all put on for the occasion;   there were no feelings of the sort at the Winchester Match, and at Henley we went out of our way to seek out and hob-nob with the Radley Eight. And before the first Great War I doubt if it ever crossed the mind of either Masters or Boys that a passionate, blind devotion to one's House, School, College, University or Regiment was not wholly commendable.   It certainly filled us with 'team spirit', and all the self-discipline and self-subordination which that celebrated spirit demands of those it possesses.   And it was often a very hard task-master, as any university wet-bob who has spent his winter afternoons 'tubbing' freshmen, instead of playing golf or squash-racquets or football with the happy dry-bobs, knows well.   But since the Great Wars, and the spectacle of, say, the Hitler Youth possessed, body and soul, by a Dark Angel, doubts have arisen.   If to Persia and Egypt and the peoples of Asia it is always 'Lord's', and Great Britain is eternally Harrow, have our own blind loyalties set no example in the matter?   One hesitates long before criticising a spirit which prompted a Persian pimp who (as Mr. Christopher Sykes has told us) only imagined himself to have been at Balliol, to prefer poverty to easy wealth because 'no Balliol man could take a bribe'.   And it is a commonplace that the honour and good name of his regiment, rather than the idea of making the world safe for democracy, has held many a soldier to his duty in battle.   Paradoxically, the self-love which shouts 'Kindersley's' from the muddy side-lines of the Field, and 'Well played, Eton!' from the box-seat of a coach at

Lord's, can and does blossom into self-sacrifice. There is a real dilemma, but Eton in my time did not know it. She must know it by now, but I doubt whether, even knowing it, she is shouting 'Well played the World!'

My own ambitions and successes at Eton lay on the River, but, looking back over the years, it is not as the scene of races won and lost that I picture that shining stream, but as my comforter and refuge in doubtful, uneasy days. For had it been possible for me to be unhappy at Eton, my second Summer Half could well have brought me to that pass. I had suddenly shot up and badly outgrown my strength; I was muscularly weak and could be put on the floor by Jackson, still a Lower boy; I was awkward and gangling, with wrists and ankles sticking out from tight clothes which were yet too new to be brought to the notice of the over-draft; I had been invited to share a 'perfect' with a much older boy, on the strength of last year's Lower Boy Pulling, and been beaten in the first round; I was called 'Sally' after a celebrated chipanzee at the Zoo whom I resembled; and, at odds with my weakness, my clothes, and my failure as an oarsman, I often 'lost my hair' and was very properly baited for it. A dry-bob, in like plight, has no escape from his companions or his own clumsiness; his games exhibit his ineptitude, and he suffers from that worst of solitudes, being with, but not of, a crowd. Being a wet-bob, I was more fortunate. On the river one could be alone, and imperceptibly, by trial and error, achieve those habits of touch and balance which in the end became as automatic as instincts. The art of oarsmanship is one thing, and has to be taught by coaches, but watermanship is quite another, and can only be self-taught; and it was during

this summer of overgrown coltishness on land that I
learned, paradoxically, through sheer length of hours
spent in a fixed-seat outrigger, to be one with my boat
as a good rider is one with his horse. I became a budding waterman, and found solace for my many inade-
quacies in the private exhilaration of developing a new
skill. And only wet-bobs will remember, with me, the
mingled smells of river-water and fresh varnish on
'Rafts'; the fine manners of Mr. Winter, the boat-
owner, who treated every Lower boy who paid for the
'chance' of a whiff as if he were the Captain of the
Boats; the racy gossip of Jack May and 'Froggy' the
boatmen ('Was the body much decomposed when you
found it, Jack?' 'Lor', you could 'ave sucked 'im
through a straw!'); and the satisfaction of bringing
alongside the fragile sculling-boat with a deft, instinct-
ive exactitude.   Once the great view of Windsor
Castle and the Brocas clump has been left behind, the
reach of the Thames on which we rowed is not a
beautiful one; past Hester's Shed and Sandbanks and
Upper and Lower Hope and Athens to Boveney Locks
there are but occasional fringes of willows on one bank
and flat fields on the other, but water is water, in sunshine or shadow, and flowing water is better still. The
very noises of rowing are a pleasure; the lapping at the
bows and the regular creak of the rowlocks take the
place, for us wet-bobs, of the summer sounds of bat
on ball; and with growing skill came the delight in
rhythmical movement which dancers know. We had
blisters and boils and actually bleeding behinds to contend with — I have been stuck by blood to my bench
in school — but there was, at long last, the 'poetry of
motion' which so charmed de Havvy. We may have

spent our long summer afternoons up and down a dull
reach, but our boat was a living thing upon water
livelier still.

Why is it that idle hours of lounging in sunshine
come back to one across the years more vividly than
the triumphs and excitements which once held all one's
attention on the stretch? So I, at any rate, find it, and
it was in this same Summer Half, before the exacting
days of constant training and racing, that Bonn and
Browning and Charrington and I sun-bathed on the
warm shaven lawns at Athens, eating black cherries
from a paper bag. We flicked each other with the
stinging tails of wet towels, and, if unlucky, were
leaped upon and ducked by Pender major, who, from
another House, did not know us by, but disliked us at,
sight. But we enjoyed the freedom of the obscure,
and were still scugs enough to buy chocolate-cream
bars and 'squashed-fly' biscuits from the Joby who
lurked with his baskets by our pathway as we trailed
lazily home through pockets of hot air. My ambitions
were still fixed, but I had to wait for more muscle, and
although my companions mostly made a butt of me,
these sun-drenched interludes put them into friendly
moods, and reconciled me to my uneasy, and socially
precarious, existence.

Our horizons, it must be admitted, were not spacious.
Except for the Boer War, public affairs were the concern of no boy that I can remember save Hugh O'Neill,
who was never a boy at all. He was reputed to read
the whole of *The Times* daily before Chapel; he had
all the gravity and aloof dignity of a future Speaker of
the Ulster House of Commons; and when the Eight
dined at the Mansion House with the first Etonian to

become Lord Mayor, Sir Joseph Dimsdale, O'Neill
spoke, broad-ribboned pince-nez in hand, with an ease
and maturity of manner which astonished the older
guests. But O'Neill was a rare bird, and when the rest
of us debated, in our House libraries or in 'Pop', on
social or political questions, we were for the most part
deplorably empty of matter. A little book called *Pros
and Cons* supplied most of the arguments on both sides.
Present Etonians, to judge from the reports of debates
in the *Chronicle*, are far more adult-minded than we
were. But they must remember that we were well
accustomed to see, in an open carriage behind two
cockaded outriders, the nodding head of a little old
lady who was Queen Victoria; that our Empire was the
Empire of Kipling's 'Recessional'; that Gladstone was
dead, Lord Rosebery in retreat, and Campbell-Banner-
man a dirty pro-Boer; that Lord Salisbury's great bulk
still brooded over us; that Joe was our man, and A. J. B.
a fine flower of Eton, flanked by her finest flower of all,
Alfred Lyttelton. Everything in the greater world was
safe, permanent, and in the best of hands; the working
classes knew their place, and our servants knew theirs
(which was in attics and basements); and if abroad
the Kaiser had been cheeky, Grandmama was entirely
capable of snubbing him as he deserved. Fear, public
fear, was unknown to us; so was uncertainty. As
young Britons living in the shadow of Windsor Castle,
we could afford to be boys and no more than boys, and
had we bothered, as we never did, to look out at the
great world, we should have seen there nothing so
exciting as our own affairs. Browning's advice to us
to buy some string at Herbert's Supply Stores, because
that counter was being served by the prettiest girl ever

seen, was more significant, as the first touch on our
cheeks of a rising wind, than anything that O'Neill
could have told us after reading *The Times*.

I went with a friend to buy string, and although I
have forgotten how pretty the young saleswoman was,
I recollect that she giggled and betrayed a perfect
awareness that it was not for string that we had crossed
the High Street from our own prescribed side to Herbert's Supply Stores. This embarrassed me, and I did
not go again; but none the less must probably date
from about this time my conversion from the view,
strongly held, that young women were odious creatures.
For my Christmas and Easter holidays were still spent
at Valescure, and after crossing, for cheapness, from
Newhaven to Dieppe, and arriving with the sick headache which in those days went with all my journeys,
I sometimes found that my mother had offered my
services as a teacher of bicycling to stray young ladies.
For in those days people were not born, as nowadays,
knowing how to bicycle; and I had to meet strange
girls by appointment on the Grand Boulevard, and to
run beside their machines while I held the saddle in a
firm grip, and exhorted them to turn the front wheel
to whichever side they felt themselves to be falling.
They always wore kid gloves, and it was the smell of
these kid gloves, which often came clinging round my
neck when the creatures' nerves failed them, that I particularly detested. Moreover they got very hot in their
long tweed skirts and gaiters, and were unfair about it
if I let them fall. I had a real distaste for girls. But
although the pretty string-seller had embarrassed me, I
had seen and felt the point of Browning's advice, and
when our new Rector's sister, Vi Labouchere, asked

me to tea and tennis at Datchet, my conversion was
complete. For Vi Labouchere was lovely to look at,
with a mouth that revealed to me in a flash why lovers
kiss, and she had a gaiety and wit and a natural flirta-
tiousness which gave to all her commerce, even with a
boy of fifteen, even at her parents' tea-table, the feel of
a love-affair. She was enchanting, in the literal sense
of the word, and I was bewitched. I longed to shine
before her, but the day was very hot, and after playing
several sets of tennis, I went, drenched with sweat, to
sit for a breather with the elders in the shade. When
I got up from my chair, there was a small pool of water
in the concave wooden seat. I saw her father eye it
with a dubious expression; whether my enchantress
saw it, I do not know, but my shame was acute, and
the memory of that humiliation shadowed, for several
years, my reveries about Vi. Still, she had done her
work with me, and when at eighteen I went, in the
holidays, to stay at the Villa Champfleuri at Cannes,
and there met Irene Murray, I was ripe for falling, and
did fall, in love. Vi had been a witch, but Irene was a
bright fellow-creature, seemingly unconscious of her
fair beauty, using no 'métier de femme', a mistress of
repartee, light-footed, laughing like Lalage. But her
voice, more like Mother Eve's than a young girl's, with
the slightest of lazy drawls to give point to her swift
ripostes, had a warm, caressing note that belied her
frank and boyish airs. But for her voice she might have
had young men as friends; with it she could only have
lovers. I was fortunate in one thing. There was in
the party a guileless Harrovian, known as 'the Beamish
boy'. Irene made common cause with me to consume
him utterly. Little can she have guessed that I returned

to Eton to fill the margins of my note-books with
futile attempts to sketch brows and eyes and nose and
lips and little escaping curls upon a white nape. Those
were the days of 'picture' hats, and when Irene appeared
in Eton Chapel with her fair face half-shadowed in
mystery, my heart turned over. Holbech, who only
two years ago had been at Bunny Hare's, was by her
side, damn him. Not that I had any illusions, only day-
dreams. I knew well enough that I was only a schoolboy. And when her engagement was announced (but
not, God be praised, to Holbech who, good fellow as
he was, was too tangible and actual to be allowed to
mate with my love) I wished her well. But I thought,
had I been a man, Irene should have known the difference indeed.

Irene was a niece of Alfred Mulholland, who at
Eton had been that 'greatest swell on earth' of my
father's recollections, and I should be graceless if I did
not recall, in this chronicle, the many visits, high-lights
in my summer holidays, to Worlingham Hall. 'A. J.'
was a tall, gaunt, shy, laconic man, with a cold blue
eye, who spent his whole life, when not shooting, in
hitting balls of different sizes. But he was kind to, and
even interested in, me as an aspiring oarsman, and when
I shot two young September pheasants in succession,
mistaking them for partridges, he soothed my burning
shame by saying how much he would enjoy eating
them. He gave me plenty of rough shooting that I
could not otherwise have enjoyed; and shooting seemed
to me then, and for many years afterwards, the best of
all fun. I never became a good shot, but I did learn, by
the observation that comes of passionate interest, to
know the ways of game-birds, and I was enabled, in

later life, to get a keener pleasure from planning a partridge drive on my own land than from shooting in
whatever numbers, with whatever — in rare moments
of inspiration — success, the birds of other people.
Worlingham lies just within Suffolk, but so near to
Norfolk that the snipe on the marshes, and the wood
pigeon on the stubbles, and the rabbits that sat, humped
and wary, outside the rounded woods on summer
evenings, might, for all you could tell, have been
natives of Norfolk itself. They were 'the right sort',
like a Leicestershire fox.

But my chief debt to Worlingham is to have known
and loved 'A. J.'s' wife, Mabel Mulholland, my mother's
closest friend. Her delicate, tip-tilted features had the
added allure of a faint irregularity, as her speech possessed the charm of vowels slightly softened, Irish
fashion. Absurdly mated to a player of games who
adored her, but could not follow her into the rarefied
air where her spirit was most at home, she lived the
life of an amused saint. Two enormous bulls walked
her lawns 'in kingly-flashing coats', because, having
made pets of them as calves, Mab had not the heart
to part with them. Dodging the bulls was a mixed
assembly of lame dogs, the London smart set, gay youth,
the halt and the blind, and priestesses of all schools
of Higher Thought. She was too short-sighted to tell
them apart at a distance of more than two yards, and
they had to learn to catch the fun or the poetry or the
other-worldly speculations aimed at other heads than
their own. Her humour and high spirits spread a
rippling veil over her manifold charities, and she lived
a life of luxury between East Anglia, the Scottish moors,
and the wistaria-clad pergolas of Champfleuri untouched

by worldliness and untroubled by the incapacity of oil to mix with water. A child of light, she was not invariably wise in her generation, but as a friend to an adolescent boy she was incomparable. I was so conscious of her looks, her frocks, and her femininity, that I must, I think, have been, without knowing it, a little in love with her. I gained self-confidence in her society, and even that measure of self-esteem which is the basis of simplicity in personal relationships. Hers was a very civilising presence.

There was a squash-racquets court at Worlingham, in which I first felt the sensuous thrill of hitting a moving ball hard. Squash-racquets is the perfect game for wet-bobs, who cannot hope to hit hard at lawn-tennis without hitting the ball out, or at cricket without being caught on the boundary. But in an enclosed box you can slog away with utter abandon, and when, by some fluke, the timing of the stroke was right, the message transmitted from the face of the racquet through shaft, hand and arm, to the player's brain, and even to his solar plexus, is one of intense delight. There is, I believe, a wistful dry-bob somewhere lurking in the depths of most wet-bobs, aching to hit a ball; and the dry-bob in me first awoke in the Worlingham squash-court. In my last year at Eton, when as Sixth Form Praepostor (who was in those days excused morning school) I played squash with the College Praepostor in Toddy Vaughan's court while our friends were listening to the Head on Polybius, or stump-cricket with Bim Gatehouse and Harry Cumberhatch in Bunny Hare's Yard, for the first time I tasted fun, sheer joyous fun, in games. The stump we used was a professional job by Mat Wright, as resilient as a cricket-bat; the ball was of a hard, but slightly yielding composition; Hare's Yard was enclosed by brick walls; I was given an 'eye' that summer for the first and last time in my life, and could hold my own, even with boys in the Eleven, in driving half-volleys smack against the bricks. I was glad enough to win the School Sculling, but for pure bliss I recollect nothing to touch those 'after twelves' in shirt-sleeves, stump in hand.

Volleying the small, light Eton football, when the turf is dry, is another sensuous delight. I started late at football, having spent my first Winter Half with Mme Poulain, and so begun it when overgrown and clumsy, but I did well enough to play 'corner' for the School on several occasions. And while an actual game was always a serious matter, into which the idea of fun never entered, I can still recollect the anticipatory prick-ing of my ears, so to speak, at the thud, thud of School Kickabout on a short after-four in November. They had begun, and one must run to the Field; for this again was unmixed fun, unrestrained kicking of a ball which, intercepted in its fall at one, and one only, correct instant of time, responds elastically, and sends through the body of the kicker a voluptuous thrill.

There were no thrills for me in the Wall Game. Although I played for the Oppidans, and even, with a rather bad conscience, had to increase the overdraft by the price of a pair of Mixed Wall Stockings, I never properly grasped what the game was about. As a 'wall', my job was to push and heave and struggle, in padded helmet and sackcloth jerkin, for a dull, exhaust-ing hour. Somewhere below the tangle of limbs and bodies Orde K.S. was sitting on the ball and must, it

possible, be dislodged. But squeezing his head between
one's knees was no good; nothing was any good.
Orde K.S. sat on the ball until the whistle blew.
Collegers, I am sure, understand the Wall Game and
pretend, none the less, that it is a good one. Oppidans
who play outside the bully occasionally get a faint
inkling of its purpose and rules. But for a 'wall',
played only for his beef and brawn, it is nothing but a
wearisome mystery. It is probably good training for
future Civil Servants, who have to live in a tangle and
obstruct, but there is no kind of fun in it.

College Field, where the Wall Game was played,
was for all that a scene of happy memories. For it was
here that, once a week in summer 'after twelves', we
senior wet-bobs played 'Aquatics'. Aquatics is cricket
played to rules designed to allow a match to be finished
in two hours. No pads or gloves may be worn; a
player is given out if he makes a purely defensive stroke
to two balls running; and he must retire when he has
scored twenty. It is a fast and furious and exhilarating
game which kept the hidden dry-bobs in us happy.
It was a game Mr. C. M. Wells did not like even to
know about. But we challenged and beat the wet-bob
Masters at it. As skipper, I put myself on to bowl first,
and took eight wickets by the simple device of bowling
so very slowly that no batsman had the patience to wait
for the ball to arrive, but made a stroke in the air from
sheer boredom, leaving himself not quite time enough
to make a second stroke before the ball, straight and
dignified, disturbed his bails. I did not exclaim that
I would rather have taken these eight wickets than
Quebec; but I felt something of the sort. 'Aquatics'
is a game played so entirely for fun and for the pleasure

Q

of hitting, not blocking, a ball, that it is surprising that
County Captains, who have to contend against ever-
falling gate receipts, do not arrange for a number of
matches under 'Aquatics' rules. The players would
enjoy themselves so much that the public would probably flock to see them doing so. But they would have
to conceal such arrangements from the M.C.C., who
would deplore a confusion of fun with games as heartily
as the Church deplores the confusion of ethics with
religion.

Nearly all these memories of extreme enjoyment
from pursuits which had nothing to do with my main
business of rowing — and I have forgotten to mention
stump-cricket with a tennis-ball on 'Rafts', where mid-
on had to field from a dinghy in mid-stream — belonged
to my last year at Eton. Just before Christmas a batch
of us had gone up to Oxford to sit for the Balliol
scholarship examination. We were lodged in dark,
low-ceilinged 'digs' in Holywell; we bought a pipe
apiece and a square-faced bottle of whisky for two-
and-sixpence; and we sat daily in Balliol Hall with
tousled young men from Scottish grammar-schools
whose accents, dickies, and expressions of ferocious
determination astonished and a little disconcerted us.
It was our first contact with youths of our own age
whose fathers would never have been allowed an overdraft by their banks, and for whom the results of this
examination might affect their whole lives. Our first
inclination to make fun of them over our whisky was
changed in a couple of days, by the spectacle of their
seriousness and intensity, to a faintly guilty sense of our
own happy situation. For, except Daniel Macmillan
who, as Newcastle Scholar, had a reputation to keep up

(and in the event won the first Open Classical Scholarship), we were sitting only because by a moderate showing in the scholarship papers one could be excused matriculation. Nothing further depended, for us, upon what marks we got. Whether it was the effect of this light-hearted approach to the papers, or of C. K. Marten's uncanny gift of guessing what questions would be set, I was awarded the Brackenbury Exhibition, worth sixty pounds a year, for History. As a result of this quite unlooked-for success, I went back to Eton with two more Halves in hand, and no necessity, that I could see, to do more work than would keep me comfortably afloat. As Captain of the Boats, Chairman — but not President — of 'Pop', and a member of Sixth Form, I had grandeur to enjoy, and considerable responsibilities.

If what I have now to relate should ever be read by any of the long line of Captains of the Boats who preceded and followed me, it will, I am afraid, be slightly shocking to them. As far as I could see, they have carried themselves with unaffected modesty and simplicity in their great office. They were quite aware, you would have said, of being merely schoolboys, 'swells' in the eyes of the small boys, and charged with a good deal of administrative business covering athletics as well as rowing, but with no sense of having attained any sort of summit. A little passing glory, no doubt, but one to be forgotten a few months after leaving School.

That was not my attitude of mind. I knew, of course, that outwardly I must be modest and unaffected. My fear, indeed, of seeming to be pleased with myself led me once into an appalling 'gaffe'. I still become hot with shame when I recollect the episode of the 'notes'. On returning to Eton from Balliol with that surprising Exhibition, I found in my room half a dozen notes from Masters — some of them, like Mr. Cyril Alington, the Master in College, unknown to me personally — with kind congratulations. I was delighted with, and treasured, these notes. But I thought that to reply to them would be a sign of self-importance. I did nothing. I did not even thank verbally those Masters whom I knew. What an oaf they must have thought me! Such are the pitfalls of adolescent self-consciousness. But inwardly, I magnified my grandeur and savoured it to the last drop of sweetness. It had been my fixed ambition for six years to be where I then stood. Even before coming to Eton my imagination had been fired by the phrase 'the greatest swell on earth'. I had not in the least been discouraged by the patent fact that my immediate predecessors had not been the greatest swells at Eton. Various cricket and football heroes had easily surpassed them. That was their own affair. Having felt myself since early childhood 'born to command', I knew that I was now indeed on a summit. It was not so much glory that I tasted, as power. I did not, except possibly for a few moments when I was handed the Ladies' Plate at Henley to the strains of the 'Eton Boating Song', feel myself to be a Chatham or a Churchill. Mine were the meaner satisfactions and gratifications of a Duke of Newcastle. It was the dispensing of patronage that I most enjoyed. It was delightful to choose the casual, the most unexpected moment at which to lift a fellow-creature suddenly to the skies by telling him that he could wear his flannels, or his Upper Boat choices. Jackson, once a rival long since left behind, was in his bath when the right to wear stick-ups was given to him through the keyhole. I liked to whisper sudden glory to a boy crowding into Chapel, and to watch him trying in vain, during the sermon, to look as if nothing had happened to him. There were over seventy colours to be given in the Boats. I was the source, though not the personal dispenser, of them all. Not even Newcastle had been the fountain of honour. He was the broker for dark-blue ribands by favour of his Sovereign, but the light-blue ribands I distributed were by my own favour alone. Yet favour is hardly the word, for I prided myself on my Roman strictness. My closest friend was a bad oar, and got no promotion. There was nothing but 'damned merit' about my awards. It is pleasant to gratify people one likes, but there is something more piquant about gratifying those one dislikes. However inevitable the boon, the giver feels magnanimous. I did indulge one fantasy. I revived an old custom, fallen into desuetude, of asking the Captain of the Eleven to take an oar in the *Monarch*, the ten-oar stroked by the Captain of the Boats in the Fourth of June procession. The *Monarch* is by tradition the shelf on which are ranged senior wet-bobs of standing who never achieved skill enough to get their Lower Boats. Sixth Form Collegers were its mainstay. Guy Campbell had no difficulty in holding his own in that company. The actual propelling of the *Ark*, which was only launched once a year, was done by the Skipper and the '9th man', a proved oar who had a line drawn under his name to separate him from the goats. The veteran 'Tugs', with the Captain of the Eleven, splashed and waved their oars behind us, and we had earned our champagne by the time Boveney Meads were reached.

Such loud inward crowing of so small a cock on so exiguous a dunghill may seem almost too childish, or at any rate immature, to record. What lack of a sense of proportion, even of a sense of humour, it betrays! But I record it because, incredible as it may seem, it has in fact affected my whole life. My toy power, my miniature prestige, were so real to me, and represented so vividly in my eyes the full and final flowering of my ambitions, that I was cured once and for all, by my brief tenure of power and personal distinction alike, of any future wish for either. I had had both; and not only had I had them, but I had recognised them for what they were. I did not even have to wait for Balliol, and Strachan-Davidson, and the Dons, and the ethos of that uncommon College, and the new revealing friendships I found there, to bring me to my senses. By the end of my last Summer Half I was satiated, and would have been ready, with Belloc, to recognise the half-truth that 'laughter and the love of friends' are the only things worth winning.

Whether this was, in the long run, good or bad, I find it difficult to decide. Without a measure of honourable ambition, few men, except saints, are likely to undertake the toils and frets of public service. Ambition has almost always its part in achievement. Do I want my grandsons when, as I hope, they go to Eton, to attain such athletic distinction as might, in their case also, purge them of any desire for future public success? Perhaps they will have the humour to take boyish triumphs more lightly than I did, and to reserve for their manhood their secret aspirations. All the same, there is a credit side to my own case. It has been pleasant to

live without envies or jealousies or heart-burnings, and
to know, in one's obscure felicity, that nobody can say:
'There goes a disappointed man.'

And this I know, that it is not only when I look back
across the years that personal triumphs are seen to dis-
solve into a background of quite another sort of happiness. Even in that last year as it was passing, I became
more and more aware of the true springs of my contentment. There was the pleasure of being at one's ease
socially; of no longer fearing rebuffs; of being under
no fancied necessity to be ungracious for fear of incur-
ring the suspicion of 'sucking up'. There was the fun
of editing, and writing a great part of, the *Amphibian*,
one of those ephemeral summer journals which are apt
to bob up on the Fourth of June. Perhaps 'fun' is not
quite the right word, for I had some bad moments
over this. One of my best friends, anxious to see himself in print, waylaid me with pertinacity, pulling out
of his pocket sheafs of verses written on broad-rule.
None of these scanned, and the rhymes anticipated the
fashions of forty years later. He was deeply hurt at my
rejection of them, but he was a poet in advance of his
time, and I was not then being old-fashioned in failing
to recognise their merit.

There were teas in the back-room of Tap, where, and
not in Heaven, as Plato thought, the 'idea' of buttered
eggs is laid up. There were everlasting arguments with
Douglas Radcliffe about Jehovah, on whose behalf
he fought a gallant rear-action, not indeed admitting
defeat until his Balliol days. There was lounging in the
sunshine on the Wall; and gossiping in other people's
House Libraries after twelve. There was the amusement of rehearsing for the Fourth of June 'Speeches',

and of finding out how human and funny even Collegers can be when seen close at hand. There were
dinner-parties with Dr. Warre and de Havvy, and the
discovery that port wine, and even claret, can make
oneself feel witty and one's elders all but indiscreet.
There was the rapture of first reading, mostly in bed,
Kipling's short stories, 'Wireless' and 'The Finest Story
in the World', and 'The Tomb of his Ancestors' and
'William the Conqueror'; which had, of course, to be
shared, and was enhanced by the sharing. There were
the jokes about the Masters, the squibs passed around
in school, the mimicry, the caricatures, the attempts at
wit, at satire, at epigram, at raconteur-ship. There was
the ragging with Denys Finch-Hatton in Little Brown's
before mid-morning school. There were the Eight's
training suppers in College Hall, with beer in pewter
tankards served by the 'Holy Poker'; and the cool feel
of the polished table, and the underlying sense of
privilege, of inherited tradition, in sitting there apart,
in that ancient place. And there were the easy, un-
demanding friendships, shallow enough for the most
part and soon known for what they were when con-
trasted with the enduring ties that bind together Balliol
men, but having a part, for all that, in the education of
the heart.

All these things made for happiness. It may be, that
had I gone straight from Eton into the world to earn
my living, I should have been but poorly equipped.
But even so, I must have blessed her. For however ill-
provided the traveller, he may not be unthankful if,
when the way is rough, he can turn his eyes back again
to a place of sunshine, where a river runs, and there are
great trees, and red bricks, and a high grey chapel lifting

strong pinnacles to the sky. For the sight will warm his heart, and nobody is the worse for that.

Leaving school is the end of boyhood, and so these recollections and reflections now come to their close. Publicly and socially, the period of nineteen years which they cover had seen few changes. When we had stood, lining the roadway within the precincts of Windsor Castle, to watch the bluejackets drawing up the hill, by ropes white with pipe-clay, the coffin of Queen Victoria, and had seen the Kaiser, on foot in British uniform, notice with amusement our tardy and ragged drill in reversing arms, we had been told that it was the end of an epoch. But it was not quite the end. At the Villa Champfleuri, it is true, we were no longer excited and exhilarated by riding in the Mulhollands' Darracq, driven by the fiery Ferdinand, whose hair was long behind his chauffeur's cap, which he touched to no man, not even to his employer. It is true that I had introduced into 'Pop' the fashion of wearing 'touts' collars, those with wings, in place of the all-round, choking stick-ups which had for so long been the misery of Victorian evening dress. And King Edward the Seventh had been nearly four years on the throne; not as an Institution, but as a human being who, for all his lovableness, had once been, as my mother felt bound to disclose to us, 'rackety'. But, by and large, there had been, except for the Boer War, no great events, at home or abroad, no social disturbances to puzzle or disquiet us, or to hurry us into adulthood. From the earliest days of chivalry and romance among the clipped Cranmer yew-hedges, through the days of rat-catching and killing, of xenophobia in exile, of reconciliation to our lot in the sunshine of Provence, no breeze from the great world had ruffled the smooth, canalised flow of our existences. We had lived, as a family, to ourselves, and I, within the family, had lived to myself, not even my parents being privy to the burden I felt in a conformity imposed by affection, or to my liberation from that burden by going to school.

The recollections of a boyhood begun, say, in 1914 or 1939 would be very different from mine. For one thing, they must have covered a shorter period, since nobody, since the first Great War, can have remained a boy for nineteen years. But small beer has its place, as well as strong ale; and a conversation-piece can be enjoyed where there is no room to hang a Rubens landscape; and it may be that, in a hundred years from now, some lover of the past, turning over the sixpenny books in a second-hand bookstall, will not be displeased to discover what a childhood, and a family, and a School were like in an age when history was, for once, holding her breath, and a boy could grow up as slowly as he pleased.

THE END

PRINTED BY R. & R. CLARK, LTD., EDINBURGH